THE WOMAN'S DAY
Low-Calorie
Dessert Cookbook

THE WOMAN'S DAY

Low-Calorie Dessert Cookbook

Carol Cutler

Houghton Mifflin Company
Boston 1980

Library of Congress Cataloging in Publication Data

Cutler, Carol.
    The Woman's day low-calorie dessert cookbook.

    Includes index.
    1. Desserts.   2. Low-calorie diet—Recipes.
I. Woman's day.   II. Title.
TX773.C84   641.8'6   79–25991
ISBN 0–395–28947–5

Printed in the United States of America

This book is dedicated to patient friends and family who allowed me to serve four desserts at a meal, who did not resent invitations for only coffee and fourteen desserts, who permitted me to intrude on their menus by bringing three desserts to their dinner parties, and most important, who allowed me to feed their children desserts by the dozen. All have been generous with their comments and criticisms, especially the children.

✿ Contents

THE WOMAN'S DAY
Low-Calorie
Dessert Cookbook

✤ Introduction

DESSERTS MEAN different things to different people. To children it usually is the highlight of the meal. The English use sweets, their term for dessert, to clear the palate for the savories, such as Welsh Rabbit, that follow. The French and Italians sandwich their dessert between the cheese and fruit courses. Americans enjoy desserts mostly for the delectable lingering flavor they leave after dinner. In none of the above roles is the dessert course essential. In fact, desserts could be called superfluous. They come after the appetite has been satisfied, and few people ascribe any real nutritional value to them. But do without dessert? Perish the thought! The dessert course is fun to eat, can be pretty as a picture, and rounds out a meal beautifully. Instead of leaving the table with tastebuds still carrying meat and fish sensations, how much better to walk away with the soft note of a Strawberry Soufflé.

But today weight control is a major concern. Doctors and nutritionists are becoming increasingly alarmed about the problem of obesity. Fad diets are rightly denounced as bad for health and only fleetingly successful. It is universally agreed that careful, consistent calorie counting is the only reliable way, dull as it may seem. So where does that put those unnecessary calories taken with dessert? Under pressure, to be sure. But since few people are disciplined enough to give up sweet treats entirely, the obvious answer is to make that treat less fattening. It's not simple, however. When you take away calories, you remove much that is alluring in desserts. Without their sinfulness desserts are less attractive. The challenge, then, is to trim calories in a major way — not just a few here and there — and still produce confections that taste quite wicked. When I first confronted this problem I thought it was an impossible task. Indeed, it has been the most difficult book I have worked on. I do believe, however, that the challenge has been met, and I hope the reader will agree.

Perhaps the biggest obstacle I put in my own path was the decision to use natural sugars only. One never knows when a chemical sweetening agent will be declared capable of causing cancer and banned from the market. Thus, not a grain or a drop of artificial sweetener is used in any of the nearly two hundred recipes in this book. While testing traditional recipes, I quickly noticed that most of them call for a grossly exaggerated amount of sugar. So from many standard recipes I cut the amount of sugar by one-third to one-half and still produced sweet-tasting dishes. While taking away sugar, fat, and starch, wherever practicable, I did try to add foods of higher nutritional value such as wheat germ, yogurt, tofu, whole wheat, and sesame seeds. Even fresh pumpkin and spaghetti squash are included.

Pastries and frozen desserts posed a more complex problem. In them, both sugars and fats play essential chemical roles, helping liquids freeze smoothly and assuring tenderness and flakiness in cakes and pies. Still, I found that significant adjustments could be made. In some cases I successfully used one egg yolk (62 calories) to replace as much as two tablespoons of butter (204 calories). Often egg yolks could be left out completely and replaced by egg whites (15 calories each). Whenever there was a choice of cutting down on fat or sugar, I always eliminated the fat, because it is more than twice as caloric. Each minor change had to be tested and retested, and the book was cooking in my kitchen for a long time.

Another way of whittling away calories is to serve smaller portions. Please note that I did not say "small." The servings indicated for each following recipe are reasonable. Unfortunately, many hosts and hostesses feel it's a sign of good hospitality to overfeed guests. But it's not even good manners. Even though few

2

people are still hungry at dessert time, if a huge slab of chocolate cake is put on the table, it will probably all be eaten, or more likely stuffed in. Then the guest hates himself and vaguely resents the hostess. Using restraint in portions is not being cheap, it's being kind. On the other hand, some recipes I have seen wildly inflate the number of people who can share a dessert. Naturally, when their total calorie count is divided by a large number of diners, the per-portion figure is temptingly low — until you see the mean little servings. I have tried to be both reasonable and honest.

This book is peppered with calorie counts — for each ingredient in a recipe, the total for the complete dish, and the one that really counts: calories per serving. My figures are based on authoritative documents, the United States Department of Agriculture Handbooks No. 8 and No. 456. A great effort was made to be as exact as possible in the figures used. But because fresh foods are variable, so are the calories they contain. An oozingly ripe July strawberry will provide more calories than a pale winter hothouse version. So-called large eggs are not of uniform size and weight. Neither are apples and oranges. Thus, the USDA compiled the best figures it could, but there still may be minor caloric variations from, say, fruit to fruit. When total calorie figures were divided for servings and the result contained a fraction, I used the next higher number for decimals of .5 and over.

The reader may also notice what appear to be discrepancies in calorie counts. For example: Whereas one tablespoon of granulated sugar is listed as containing 46 calories, one cup (16 tablespoons) is a disproportionate 770. What appears to be bad multiplication (16 × 46 equals 736) is actually extremely precise weight measurement. The USDA calculates all nutritional values of foods by weight, and accordingly, one tablespoon of sugar will weigh 12 grams, but the more compact cup will be 200, not 192. (USDA Handbook No. 456, items 2230 a and b.) Also, when converting from grams to ounces, analysts rounded out fractions; thus, variances are produced in the number of calories in larger quantities. Though not perfect, these are the best figures available and are used by doctors, nutritionists, and diet clinics.

*

Until now the serious dieter who likes natural, unadulterated foods faced dessert time with a dilemma: Break the calorie bank or abstain. This book offers a pleasing third choice.

As the last taste of sweets, is sweetest last,
Writ in remembrance more than things long past.
— *William Shakespeare*

❀ Hints for Low-Calorie Dessert Preparation

- Invest in hard-surfaced, nonstick equipment, especially cake pans, frying pans, and gelatin molds.
- When painting pastry before baking to produce a glaze, use evaporated skimmed milk instead of egg yolk.
- Grease cake pans and cookie sheets with a light wiping of mineral oil. It has no intrusive taste and no calories.
- Use a stiff vegetable brush to scrape out every bit of grated orange or lemon peel clinging to the sharp teeth of small graters.
- Buy an antifreeze ice cream scoop for cutting easily through frozen desserts. It can also be used for scraping ices into fluffy servings.
- Contrary to the dictum of *nouvelle cuisine* chefs, who favor outsized plates for framing food compositions, use undersized plates and bowls so a smaller portion appears to be full.
- After adding softened gelatin to a hot sauce, pour a little of the hot liquid into the small gelatin bowl to dissolve every bit of gelatin clinging to it.
- If milk is generally put on the table for coffee, substitute chilled evaporated milk or evaporated skimmed milk; do not dilute it. Calorie counts for one teaspoon are: evaporated skimmed milk — 4; evaporated milk — 7; coffee cream — 11.

- Beaten egg whites are great calorie extenders. Here are several rules for properly handling them: They must be at room temperature to produce maximum volume. They must be free of any fat, meaning scraps of egg yolk in the whites or fat on the bowl; for this reason metal or ceramic bowls are best for beating egg whites because they do not hold fats the way porous plastic does. Do not overbeat the whites; when the peaks stand upright but fold over softly at the tips, they are ready. Hand-beating egg whites in an unlined copper bowl is the best method, because they will have more volume and be thicker, but cream of tartar added to whites beaten in bowls made of other materials provides the chemical additive given off by copper. Recipe instructions often say to fold in part of the beaten whites first, then the remainder, but always rebeat the remaining whites briefly before adding.

- When adding egg whites to a sauce base, first incorporate about one-third of the beaten whites and fold them in thoroughly. This will lighten the sauce, making it easier to fold in the rest of the whites lightly, thus breaking them down less.

- Apples considered best for eating fresh include McIntosh, Red Delicious, Golden Delicious, Cortland, Jonathan, Stayman, Winesap, Melrose, and Franklin. For applesauce and pies select Golden Delicious, McIntosh, Melrose, Cortland, York, Winesap, Stayman, and Rome Beauty.

- Bake custards in smaller-sized cups. Especially practical are 2½-inch paper-lined foil muffin-baking cups. Each holds about ½ cup, which is a good portion.

- Carefully read labels on processed foods. Producers are obliged to list ingredients in descending order of quantity contained. Very often there is more sugar than the basic food itself.

- When baking, use two sets of measuring spoons and cups, one exclusively for liquid ingredients and the other for dry.

- Be wary of packaged desserts that loudly claim "low fat." They start that way, but often are crammed with heavily sweetened fruit, fruit jams, and sugars. The low-fat claim is correct, but sugar isn't mentioned. The calorie count on the package will tell the true story.

- Count on wines and liqueurs for a lot of flavor and few calories. Once heated to 180 degrees Fahrenheit, most of the alcohol and calories burn off, leaving just a small amount of residual sugar.

- If possible, use imported fruit liqueurs. Their fruit flavors are truer and stronger. Though they cost more, only small quantities are used in cooking.

- When working with standard recipes for custards, puddings, and creams, use extra vanilla instead of a full measure of sugar. Its aromatic flavor will largely compensate for the reduced sweetness.

- Use pure vanilla. Its slightly higher cost is quickly compensated in the kitchen. There is no imitation for its deep aroma.

- In standard dessert preparations, cut down on sugar drastically. For some of the classic recipes reworked for this book it was possible to cut sugar in half.

- If a choice comes down to a tablespoon of sugar or a tablespoon of butter, go with the sugar, which has only 46 calories, versus 102 for the butter.

- Butter and margarine have exactly the same calorie count — 102 per tablespoon. If your diet permits and you need not be rigid in cholesterol control, use the butter, which gives greater flavor for the calories.

- Use cocoa instead of chocolate wherever you can. The richness of chocolate is contained in its cocoa butter, which is removed in cocoa. Carob powder also has a natural slightly chocolate flavor.

- If working with recipes that call for milk, substitute skimmed milk; use evaporated milk or evaporated skimmed milk for cream, and yogurt for sour cream.

- In general, when using crushed cereal, cookies, or graham crackers in recipes, compensate for the extra sugar they contain by reducing the amount of sugar in the rest of the recipe.

- When selecting fresh fruit to serve, pick medium-sized specimens. They generally are large enough for a healthy portion.

- When fresh fruit is served, slice it whenever possible. Less than a whole piece of fruit can still look ample.
- If sugar is used in a poaching syrup for fruit, some of the syrup can be used to sweeten purées, batters, and creams.

❧ Fruit-based Desserts

FRESH FRUIT is, of course, nature's sweet gift to dieters. When fully ripened and brimming with natural sugars, a peach, pear, melon, or bowlful of strawberries is the ultimate, pure dessert. Unfortunately, the economics of big-volume marketing have intruded upon nature to accommodate mechanical handling, long-distance transportation, and extensive storage life. But what is convenient for the grower is not always good for the consumer. Taste tells. The deterioration in the quality of mass-produced fruits and vegetables has contributed greatly to the tremendous resurgence of popularity of local farmers' markets as well as pick-your-own orchards.

But where agribusiness fails, the cook takes over. By adding a judicious amount of flavorings, the chef can bake a less-than-perfect peach into a golden orb of steaming goodness that still adds up to just over 80 calories. Similarly, an ordinary pear is wrapped in aluminum foil with just a few enhancements and emerges from the oven deliciously transformed, at the cost of only 17 extra calories.

Fruits are also stuffed, scalloped, turned into compotes, baked as a "cake," puréed into soup or mousse, and even skewered for a kebab. Vegetables have also found their way into this chapter. Pumpkin Surprise is just that — a baked-in-the-shell confection that no Hallowe'en goblin has ever encountered. Nor could I resist working with that strangest of all vegetables, the spaghetti squash. Yes, it can be a dessert, an intriguing orange-flavored one.

Here are several dozen fruit-based recipes that finish a meal elaborately without breaking the calorie bank.

❀ Baked Apples

total calories — 428 • per serving — 71

Next to apple pie, baked apple is probably the universal American dessert, and rightly so. The apple season is a long one and the preparation of the fruit could not be easier. Usually, though, the natural goodness of the fruit is overwhelmed by fillings of cloying sweetness that can add an extra burden of anywhere from 60 to 80 extra calories. This version avoids such excesses by adding only three surprisingly compatible flavorings that add up to a mere 10 calories per serving.

Serves 6

5	teaspoons sweetened, flaked coconut	(35)
½	teaspoon powdered ginger	(3)
6	medium apples	(366)
6	teaspoons dark rum	(24)

Preheat oven to 350°.

1. Toss the coconut and ginger together in a small bowl to blend the two thoroughly. Remove the stem and core of the apples, but do not cut all the way to the bottom. A grapefruit knife is perfect for this task. Divide the spiced coconut among the apples, loosely filling each center cavity. Pour 1 teaspoon of rum into each apple.

2. Place the apples in a baking dish and pour in water to a ¼-inch depth. Cover and place the dish in the preheated oven and bake until soft. (Count on 40 to 50 minutes depending on the quality of the fruit.) For the last 10 minutes of baking, remove the cover to allow the apple skins to crisp slightly.

3. Serve warm — not piping hot — or cold.

✿ Apple Compote

total calories — 839 • *per serving — 105*

This dish is a far cry from applesauce. The fruit is sliced and baked and given a zesty taste with just a minimum of different flavorings.

Serves 8

1 teaspoon butter	(34)
3 pounds apples, preferably Stayman, York, or Rome Beauty (about 12 or 13)	(735)
rind of 1 lemon	——
1 tablespoon brown sugar	(34)
3 tablespoons orange liqueur	(36)
Optional: whipped evaporated skimmed milk flavored with orange liqueur (page 204)	

Preheat oven to 325°.

1. Butter an 8-cup soufflé or similar baking dish. Peel the apples, quarter them, remove the cores, and slice thin.

2. With a swivel-bladed vegetable peeler, remove the rind from the lemon; chop it fine. Put one-third of the apples in the baking dish, then sprinkle on one-third of the lemon peel, 1 teaspoon brown sugar, and 1 tablespoon of the liqueur. Repeat two more times.

3. Cover the dish closely with aluminum foil and bake for about 1½ hours. The apples will be very soft but will still maintain their shape. Serve warm, but not hot. If the optional whipped skimmed milk is used, pass it separately.

✿ Baked Apple Cup

calories per 1-cup serving — 109

The single person dining alone often has a dessert dilemma: Either eat a ready-made confection that is generally high in calories and low in good natural flavors or have a piece of fruit and let it go at that. There are other easy solutions, and this is one of them. Baked Apple Cup can be prepared right in the baking dish, thus saving some wash-up time. Also, it is especially good when warm and so can be enjoyed shortly after preparation. If placed in the oven just before beginning dinner, the dessert will be ready when you are. As good as it is the first day, you will also find these cups of dessert equally enjoyable when well chilled, and the applesauce is of firmer consistency. To encourage deliberate leftovers, or for an easy treat when company comes, proportions are also given for 6 servings.

Serves 1

¼	small apple	(10)
1	teaspoon dark rum	(4)
1	teaspoon orange juice	(2)
½	cup unsweetened applesauce	(50)
⅛	teaspoon ground coriander	——
⅛	teaspoon vanilla	——
½	teaspoon cornstarch	(5)
2	tablespoons plain low-fat yogurt	(16)
2	teaspoons dark brown sugar	(22)

Serves 6

1 medium apple
2 tablespoons dark rum
2 tablespoons orange juice
3 cups unsweetened applesauce
scant teaspoon ground coriander
scant teaspoon vanilla
1 tablespoon cornstarch
¾ cup plain low-fat yogurt
¼ cup dark brown sugar

Preheat oven to 350°.

1. Peel, core, and slice the apple thin. Place it in a small bowl and sprinkle on the rum and orange juice (or double the amount of orange juice and omit the rum). Turn the slices with your hands to make certain that each one is coated with the liquid. Cover and put aside for 15 minutes.

2. Meanwhile, stir together the applesauce, coriander, vanilla, and cornstarch, and spoon into 1-cup baking dishes. (For an individual portion, stir the above ingredients together in the baking dish.) Lift the apple slices from the marinade and arrange them over the applesauce, then dribble the marinade over the apples.

3. Measure the yogurt into the marinade bowl and beat in the brown sugar until well blended. Spoon the yogurt over the apple slices and bake in the preheated oven for 30 minutes, or until the apples are tender when pierced with a small, sharp knife.

4. To serve: Place each cup on a saucer along with a teaspoon. This dessert is best eaten warm or well chilled, not hot.

❀ Danish Apple Cake

total calories — 1064 • per serving — 133

Danish pastry means much, much more than that sticky American breakfast bun, which is something else again in its homeland. The teatime break is also a Danish ritual that provides another opportunity to indulge in those justly famous pastries. This Danish apple dessert comes in cake form, but it really consists of layers of cooked fruit and crumbs all baked together. Crushed zwieback biscuits are used instead of the traditional buttered bread crumbs, since those soft crumbs can sponge up an awesome amount of fat. The final taste, however, is still traditionally *godt*.

Serves 8

2	pounds apples (about 8), preferably York or Cortland	(490)
¼	cup water	——
2	tablespoons granulated sugar	(96)
	rind ½ orange, grated	——
8	zwieback biscuits, crumbled (about ¾ cup)	(240)
2	tablespoons brown sugar	(68)
½	teaspoon cinnamon	(3)
2	tablespoons jelly, currant or raspberry	(102)
2	tablespoons apple juice	(14)
½	tablespoon butter	(51)

13

Preheat oven to 350°.

1. Peel the apples, core them, and cut into chunks. Place the apple pieces in a saucepan, pour in the water, cover, and simmer for about 20 to 25 minutes, or until the apples are completely soft. Mash them by hand or in a food processor, but do not work them until entirely smooth. Stir in the granulated sugar and grated orange rind.

2. In a bowl, stir together the zwieback crumbs, brown sugar, and cinnamon. Meanwhile, in a very small pot or butter melter combine the jelly and apple juice and place on low heat to melt the jelly.

3. Butter a 6-cup soufflé dish or similar mold and alternate layers of the crumbs, apple purée, and melted jam. Finish with a sprinkling of jelly over the crumbs. Place in the oven and bake for 35 to 40 minutes, or until a knife plunged in the center comes out rather dry. Serve warm.

❀ Pommes Enrobées
(Apples Baked in Crumb Crust)

total calories — 783 • per serving — 131

As a novelty treat try these baked apples with a packaging difference. This preparation also solves the dilemma of those who can't decide if they should eat the skin or not.

Serves 6

6 medium apples, preferably Stayman, York, or McIntosh	(318)
2 tablespoons butter, melted	(204)
½ cup graham cracker crumbs	(163)
2 teaspoons cocoa	(10)
½ teaspoon nutmeg	(6)
2 gingersnaps	(58)
1 tablespoon rum	(12)
6 miniature marshmallows	(12)
Optional: whipped evaporated skimmed milk (page 204)	

Preheat oven to 350°.

1. Peel the apples and remove the core. Be careful not to cut into the bottom of the apple; a grapefruit knife works well. Melt the butter while mixing together in a small bowl the crumbs, cocoa, and nutmeg. Spread some of the seasoned crumbs on a sheet of wax paper or a dish.

2. With a brush, paint each apple with the melted butter. Immediately roll it in the crumbs, patting to make them adhere better. As each apple is coated, place it on a baking dish. Add more crumbs to the wax paper or dish as needed.

3. Crumble the ginger snaps into coarse bits and use to fill the hollowed-out cores. Pour about a ½ teaspoon of rum into each center and top with a marshmallow. If any melted butter remains, dribble it over the apples.

4. Bake the apples for about 30 minutes, or until soft when tested with a small, sharp knife. Serve very warm, but not piping hot. If the optional whipped skimmed milk is used, pass it separately.

❀ Apple "Cake"

total calories — 872 • per serving — 145
with 1 tablespoon dessert sauce — 165

This well-chilled apple "cake" really isn't a cake at all. Soft sautéed apple slices are pressed into a soufflé dish and refrigerated to allow the small amount of butter and sugar to bind the separate pieces into one lovely whole. It is served cold with, unexpectedly, a hot sauce.

Serves 6

2 pounds apples (7 or 8), preferably Stayman, York, or McIntosh	(490)
2 tablespoons butter	(204)
¼ cup brown sugar	(136)
½ teaspoon nutmeg	(6)
3 tablespoons dark rum	(36)
1 cup Creamy Dessert Sauce (page 195)	

1. Peel, quarter, core, and slice the apples thin. Place them in a wide skillet and dot with the butter cut into pieces. Sprinkle with the sugar, nutmeg, and rum and place uncovered on medium heat.

2. Cook the apples until they are soft and slightly transparent, about 15 minutes. Turn occasionally with a wooden spoon, taking care not to crush the apples; the slices should remain distinct, not mashed, and the liquid should be absorbed by the fruit. Remove from the heat and cool.

3. When the apples are lukewarm, place them in a lightly oiled 6-cup soufflé dish. Since the cake will be reversed for serving, make an attractive pattern of the slices on the bottom of the dish. Press down firmly on the apples. Refrigerate overnight, or for at least 3 hours.

4. Remove the dessert from the refrigerator about 30 minutes before serving. Loosen the edges with a small knife and lightly lift the bottom of the cake. Dip the dish in hot water, or reverse it onto the serving platter and place a hot towel on the bottom of the dish for a few seconds. Holding them together, sharply shake the soufflé dish and platter to release the cake. Spoon the hot dessert sauce over the top.

✿ Caramel Apples
total calories — 610 • per serving — 102

Thanks to the forthright flavor of caramel, a small amount of it can replace generous globs of cream and butter. That is the stratagem employed here — freshly baked apples are enriched with a little hot caramel just before going to the table. Low in calories, indeed, but very high in eating pleasure.

Serves 6

6 *medium apples, preferably Golden Delicious*	(318)
1 *teaspoon butter*	(34)
1 *tablespoon dark brown sugar*	(34)
2 *tablespoons dark rum*	(24)
2 *tablespoons lemon juice*	(8)
¼ *cup granulated sugar*	(192)

16

Preheat oven to 375°.

1. Peel the apples and carefully cut out the cores; a grapefruit knife accomplishes this easily. Place the apples on a buttered baking dish that will hold them snugly. Fill each cavity with ½ teaspoon of brown sugar, 1 teaspoon of rum, and 1 teaspoon of lemon juice. Pour about ¼ cup of cold water into the baking dish and place in the oven. Bake, uncovered, until the apples have browned a little, about 30 minutes; baste several times.

2. Cover the baking dish with a lid or a piece of aluminum foil and return to the oven for another 15 or 20 minutes, or until the fruit is soft when pierced with a sharp knife.

3. When the apples are ready, turn off the oven but do not remove the baking dish. Put the granulated sugar in a small, heavy pot with 1 tablespoon of cold water. Place the pot on medium-high heat and let it simmer until the sugar takes on a nutty brown color; do not stir the sugar, but rotate the syrup by shaking the pan. A lightly caramelized sugar should take only 1 or 2 minutes; watch it carefully, because caramel can burn quite easily.

4. Place the apples on warm dessert dishes and pour a little hot caramel over each one. Serve immediately.

❀ Caramelized Apple Slices
total calories — 910 • per serving — 152

The long baking of this excellent winter dessert insures a steady caramelizing of the apple slices without the usual overpowering amount of sugar, often as much as three cups. With this method the tangy caramel flavor penetrates every tender morsel of apple. Consider this a company dessert, too, despite its simplicity.

Serves 6

½	cup sugar	(385)
6	tablespoons water	——
2	pounds (7 or 8) apples, preferably York or McIntosh	(490)
1	teaspoon nutmeg	(11)
2	tablespoons rum	(24)

Preheat oven to 350°.

1. Put 2 tablespoons of sugar in a straight-sided metal charlotte mold or a small enameled cast-iron casserole that holds about 2 quarts. Sprinkle 1 tablespoon of water over the sugar and place on medium heat. If using a charlotte mold, place it on a heat-deflector pad. Without stirring, melt the sugar and let it caramelize to a dark nutty brown. Watch it carefully as it browns, since it can turn from caramel to burnt sugar in a flash. The whole process takes less than 2 minutes. Using 2 heavy pot holders, immediately lift the pan and swirl it quickly to coat the mold with caramel. Put aside to cool and harden while the apples are prepared.

2. Peel, quarter, core, and slice the apples thin. Divide the apples, nutmeg, and remaining 6 tablespoons of sugar into three layers in the caramelized mold. Before adding the final coating of nutmeg and sugar, press down firmly with your hands on top of the apples. Dribble over the top 1 tablespoon of rum.

3. Put the mold in a pan containing water that reaches to one-third its depth and place in the oven for 2 hours, basting occasionally with a bulb baster. (If the oven is being used for other preparations, the apples will profit by an extra 30 minutes of baking.) Remove the mold from the oven and let the dessert cool for about 20 minutes. Use a spatula to pull the cooked apples away from the edges of the mold, at the same time lifting the bottom lightly. Place a serving dish over the top of the mold and reverse the compactly shaped apples onto it.

4. Pour the remaining 5 tablespoons of water and 1 tablespoon of rum into the metal mold, place over high heat, and boil rapidly for about a half-minute to dissolve the caramel clinging to the pan. Pour this hot syrup over the apples and serve while still warm.

❀ Banana Mousse

total calories — 307 • per serving — 77
with banana garnish — 86 • with cocoa garnish — 79

Banana Mousse is a quickly prepared dessert. From peeling the banana to the table, the mousse can be ready in a half-hour if chilled in the freezer. Each serving is only 11 calories more than plain low-fat yogurt — but what an 11 calories.

Serves 4

2 tablespoons skimmed milk	(12)
1 teaspoon kirsch	(12)
1 teaspoon vanilla	(6)
1 tablespoon sugar	(46)
1 medium banana	(101)
1 cup plain low-fat yogurt	(130)
Optional: 8 thin banana slices or cocoa for garnish	

1. Place in the container of an electric blender or food processor the skimmed milk, kirsch, vanilla, sugar, and the banana broken into chunks. Process until the banana has been puréed. There should be 1 cup of purée; if not, add another piece or two of banana. Pour the purée into a mixing bowl.
2. Fold the yogurt into the purée and chill well.
3. To serve: Spoon the Banana Mousse into four serving dishes and, if desired, garnish either with 2 slices of banana on each dish or a light sprinkling of cocoa.

❀ Stuffed Bananas

total calories — 599 • per serving — 150

Bananas seem to have a natural affinity for rum, a liaison that is capitalized on here. Anytime you feel you can spare an extra 5 to 10 calories a portion, sprinkle a few chopped nuts over the stuffing.

Serves 4

4	medium bananas	(404)
½	cup rum	(93)
2	tablespoons powdered sugar	(58)
¼	teaspoon cinnamon	(2)
2	teaspoons vanilla	(12)
2	egg whites, room temperature	(30)

1. Rinse and wipe the unpeeled bananas, then slit each one the entire length of the curved inside. Carefully remove the banana pulp with a teaspoon and place the pulp in a bowl. Put the banana skins in a plastic bag and refrigerate until needed for stuffing; this will keep them from turning dark brown.

2. Bring ¼ cup rum to a boil in a small pot, remove, and cool. Mash the banana pulp, and once it has been fairly well broken up, continue mashing while adding the sugar. When the pulp is quite smooth, add the boiled rum, cinnamon, and vanilla. Cover and put in a cool spot for 1 or 2 hours, stirring from time to time.

Preheat the oven to 375°.

3. Beat the egg whites until they are very firm and delicately fold them into the banana mixture. Spread each banana skin and fill with the mixture. Reclose the slits a little. Place the stuffed bananas on a nonstick or lightly greased baking dish that will hold them snugly. Bake for 10 to 12 minutes, or until the filling has puffed nicely and turned a light brown.

4. Heat the remaining ¼ cup of rum, pour over the bananas, and ignite it with a match. Serve at once.

❈ Melon Dessert Soup

total calories — 415 • per serving — 69
with melon garnish — 77

Fruit soups are a staple in Scandinavia. Americans, however, tend to shy away from them, largely because we are never sure just when to serve them. By adding a good dash of liqueur it definitely has its proper place as dessert. Cantaloupe is especially good handled this way.

Serves 6

4	cups melon cut in pieces (about 2 lb.)	(192)
1	cup plain low-fat yogurt	(130)
½	cup orange juice	(54)
1	tablespoon lemon juice	(4)
1	tablespoon amaretto or orange liqueur	(35)
	Optional: 1 cup chilled melon balls or fresh mint sprigs for garnish	

1. Combine all ingredients except the garnish in a blender or food processor and purée to a smooth consistency. Chill.
2. To serve: Spoon the dessert soup into individual soup cups and garnish with several melon balls or the mint sprig, if desired.

❀ Cantaloupe Ambrosia

total calories — 310 • per serving — 78

This melon recipe differs from the preceding Melon Soup in that the cantaloupe is not puréed to a thoroughly smooth consistency. Nor is it as thin. Cantaloupe Ambrosia is pure fruit and yogurt. That's it. Add sugar only if the melon is of inferior quality.

Serves 4

4	cups melon cut in pieces (about 2 lb.)	(192)
¾	cup plain low-fat yogurt	(96)
1	tablespoon sweetened, flaked coconut	(22)

1. Put the melon and yogurt in a blender or food processor and process briefly, just until the melon has been cut into small pieces. Do not purée until smooth. Pour the melon into 4 dessert bowls and chill. (If ingredients are already cold, the dessert can be served immediately.)

2. Lightly toast the coconut in a hot oven or under the broiler. If using the broiler, do not take your eyes off the coconut. In either case, turn the flakes several times. Cool.

3. To serve: Sprinkle a little of the toasted coconut over the bowls of melon.

❀ Nectarines à la Nectarine

total calories — 646 • per serving — 108

There is no reason this recipe can't be changed to Pêches à la Pêche (peaches), Ananas à l'Ananas (pineapple), or Poires à la Poire (pears). The purity of the dessert is maintained by using the same fruit twice — in slices and for the purée to pour over them.

Serves 6

6 nectarines	(528)
2 tablespoons kirsch	(24)
2 teaspoons sugar	(30)
½ cup plain low-fat yogurt	(64)
Optional: fresh mint sprigs for garnish	

1. Peel 2 nectarines, cut into chunks, and purée in a blender or food processor. Pour the purée into a small, heavy pot, add the kirsch and sugar, and place on medium heat. Cook, stirring the fruit until it has warmed through thoroughly and the sugar has dissolved. Transfer the purée to a mixing bowl. When it is cool, stir in the yogurt until completely blended. Chill.

2. At serving time, peel the remaining 4 nectarines, slice, and divide them among 6 dessert dishes. Spoon 3 tablespoons of the chilled purée over each portion. The optional mint garnish can be placed on top.

❀ Sliced Orange Compote

total calories — 865 • per serving — 144

This is another instance where half the usual quantity of sugar is eliminated and the final results are just as good. Part of the reason less sugar works is that not one drop of orange juice is lost while slicing the fruit; all of it must go into the bowl. Secondly, orange liqueur is used with a liberal hand because its alcohol boils off, leaving only the residual sugar, which is not as much as you'd think.

Serves 6

6	good-quality seedless oranges	(384)
2	cups water	——
½	cup sugar	(385)
¼	teaspoon freshly grated nutmeg	(3)
½	cup orange liqueur	(93)

1. With a swivel-bladed vegetable peeler, carefully remove the rind from the oranges, making certain that none of the white underskin is included. Cut the rind into very, very thin juliennes. Meanwhile, bring the water, sugar, and nutmeg to a boil. Add the orange strips and simmer, partially covered, for 15 minutes.

2. During this time, cut away the white part of the peel from the oranges. Cut the oranges across in even ¼-inch slices on a cutting board with juice grooves or a saucer. As you work, place the slices in a deep bowl that can withstand boiling syrup. Scrape into the bowl any juice that collects on the cutting board.

3. Pour the orange liqueur into the boiling syrup, let simmer for a half-minute, then pour the syrup over the orange slices through a strainer that will catch the orange rind strips. Remove ½ cup of the cooking syrup to a small pot. Closely cover the orange slices at once, let cool completely at room temperature, then chill.

4. Add the drained orange rind to the small pot with the half-cup of syrup. Put over medium heat and cook, uncovered, until all the liquid has evaporated and the strips are lightly caramelized. Scrape them into a small bowl, cover, and refrigerate.

5. To serve: Transfer 4 or 5 orange slices to a dessert plate, spoon a little of the syrup over them, then garnish with a little of the caramelized orange rind.

❀ Baked Peaches

total calories — 486 • per serving — 81

Good peaches in season need little embellishment. Unfortunately, the fruit is often less than perfect. Baking provides a simple and easy way to make the most of what you have. Superior peaches, on the other hand, produce superior results.

Serves 6

¼	cup sugar	(192)
¼	cup water	——
¼	teaspoon cinnamon	(2)
½	teaspoon freshly grated nutmeg	(6)
2	tablespoons orange liqueur	(24)
1	teaspoon butter	(34)
6	ripe peaches	(228)
	Optional: ½ cup Strawberry Sauce (page 196)	

Preheat oven to 350°.

1. Put sugar, water, cinnamon, and nutmeg together in a small, heavy pot and boil rapidly on high heat for 10 minutes. Add the orange liqueur and simmer 1 minute more. Remove the pot from the fire and add the butter.

2. Meanwhile, plunge the peaches into boiling water for a few seconds. Lift them out with a slotted spoon and slip off the skins. Place the peaches in a baking dish that has a cover (lacking a cover use aluminum foil). Pour the syrup on the peaches, cover, and bake for about 20 minutes, or until the peaches are soft when tested with a sharp knife. Baste several times during the baking.

3. Serve hot. If you like, pass the cold Strawberry Sauce, which makes a pretty color combination.

❦ Pêches Enrobées
(Peaches Baked in Crumb Crust)

total calories — 598 • per serving — 100
with whipped milk — 107

Certainly peaches can be baked whole and plain, as in the preceding recipe. But by cashing in just a few extra calories they become quite something else again — a pretty toothsome parcel.

Serves 6

6 peaches	(228)
2 tablespoons butter	(204)
½ cup graham cracker crumbs	(163)
½ teaspoon cinnamon	(3)

Optional: ½ cup whipped evaporated skimmed milk (page 204)

Preheat oven to 350°.

1. Bring a pot of water to a boil and plunge in the peaches. Keep the peaches in the water for about 10 seconds if ripe, a bit longer if they are hard. Remove the peaches with a slotted spoon and as soon as they are cool enough to handle, slip off the skins.

2. Meanwhile, melt the butter in a very small pot. Mix the graham cracker crumbs and cinnamon together in a small bowl. Prepare either a sheet of wax paper or a dish and pour a few tablespoons of the seasoned crumbs onto it.

3. With a brush, paint each peach with the melted butter; then immediately roll it in the crumbs, patting to make them adhere better. As each peach is coated, place it on a baking dish or in individual scallop shells. If scallop shells are used, place them on a baking sheet. Repeat with the other peaches, adding more crumbs to the wax paper or dish as needed. If any melted butter remains, dribble it over the peaches.

4. Bake for 15 to 25 minutes, depending on the ripeness of the fruit. Test by piercing with a small, sharp knife; the fruit should be soft.

5. Serve the whole baked peaches very warm, but not piping hot. If the optional whipped skimmed milk is used, pass it separately.

✿ Poires en Chemise
(Pears Baked in Foil Packages)
per serving — 112

Whether you are making a single portion of dessert or for a group, this is one recipe that adapts well. Ingredients are listed for one serving and for six.

Serves 1

aluminum foil	
1 pear	(95)
1 teaspoon sugar	(15)
1 teaspoon lemon juice	(1)
1 or 2 drops of vanilla	———
¼ teaspoon orange liqueur or kirsch	(1)

Serves 6

aluminum foil
6 pears
2 tablespoons sugar
juice of ½ lemon
½ teaspoon vanilla
1½ teaspoons orange liqueur or kirsch

Preheat oven to 375°.

1. For each pear, prepare a 10-inch-square sheet of aluminum foil. Peel the pear, leaving the stem intact and cutting a slice off the bottom so the pear will stand upright. Place the pear in the center of the foil square.

2. For the single serving, simply sprinkle the flavorings over the pear. If preparing six portions, mix the sugar, lemon juice, vanilla, and liqueur or kirsch together in a small bowl. Stir to dissolve the sugar a little, then spoon this sweet dressing over the pears.

3. Draw up the sides of the foil and close it around the pear to make a tight seal. Place the pear on a baking dish and bake for about 1 hour or until soft, depending on the ripeness of the fruit. (The single serving is best prepared when the oven is being used for some other baking, in order to save energy.)

❀ Ginger Pears

total calories — 1122 • per serving — 140

If the Chinese had a tradition for desserts, they might very well offer this one. It meets all their criteria: pretty to look at, not rich or filling, and an interesting combination of flavors.

Serves 8

SAUCE:

4	cups dry white wine	(200)
2	tablespoons sugar	(92)
	strip of orange rind, about 2 inches long	——
10	slices fresh ginger	(5)
1	tablespoon vanilla	(18)
2	teaspoons amaretto or orange liqueur	(8)

PEARS:

½	lemon	(10)
8	pears, medium-sized (about 6 or 7 ounces each)	(760)
1	tablespoon cornstarch	(29)
¼	cup water	——

1. Place all sauce ingredients in a straight-sided skillet that will hold the pears snugly. Bring the wine to a boil, reduce heat, cover, and simmer 15 minutes.

2. Meanwhile, fill a large mixing bowl with cold water, squeeze in the juice of the lemon, and toss the shell in the water. Use a swivel-bladed vegetable peeler to peel the pears, leaving the stem intact. Remove a slice from the bottom of each pear to insure that it will stand upright. Drop the pears into the acidulated water to keep them from turning brown.

3. Place the pears in the simmering syrup, cover, and poach 15 to 20 minutes, or until just soft when pierced with a small, sharp knife. Do not overcook, because after cooking the fruit will be cooled in the hot sauce and thus become softer. Timing will depend on their ripeness. Remove the pears to a bowl and discard the orange rind and ginger slices.

4. Place the cornstarch in a small cup and mix in the water, then stir into the poaching liquid with a wire whisk until the liquid begins to thicken. Reduce the heat, cover, and simmer for 5 minutes. Pour the hot sauce over the poached pears, cover the bowl, and cool. Place in refrigerator to chill.

5. Remove the bowl from the refrigerator 1 hour before serving. The flavor is better if not icy cold. Place each pear on an individual dessert dish and spoon several tablespoons of sauce over the fruit.

✤ Pears Bourdaloue

total calories — 1209 • per serving — 151

Fresh fruit figures importantly in French desserts. In season, pears come in an array of temptations. One favorite variation is Bourdaloue. Classically, the poached pears and a cream sauce are held in a pastry shell, which can account for up to an extra 1800 calories. The pastry is completely expendable when the composed dessert receives a final fillip of caramelized sugar under the broiler.

Serves 8

PEARS:

5	medium pears	(475)
1½	cups water	——
2	tablespoons sugar	(92)
1	teaspoon vanilla	(6)

SAUCE:

2	eggs	(154)
2	tablespoons sugar	(92)
1	tablespoon flour	(28)
1½	cups evaporated skimmed milk	(288)
1	teaspoon vanilla	(6)
2	tablespoons brown sugar	(68)

1. In a flat skillet, bring the water, granulated sugar, and vanilla to a boil. Meanwhile, peel, quarter, and core the pears. Add them to the syrup, cover the skillet, and simmer gently until the pears have been poached and are just soft. Depending on the ripeness of the fruit, this should take 5 to 10 minutes. Remove the pears from the syrup with a slotted spoon and drain on paper towels.

2. Break the eggs into a heavy nonaluminum saucepan and mix with the granulated sugar and flour. While beating with a whisk, pour in the evaporated skimmed milk and place on a heat-deflector pad over medium heat. Cook while stirring constantly until the sauce thickens. Do not allow it to boil. Stir in the vanilla and cook a half-minute longer. Remove from the heat and cool.

3. Spoon a thin layer of the sauce into the bottom of an 8-inch pie dish from which the dessert can be served. Arrange the well-drained pears over the sauce and cover them completely with the remaining sauce. Sprinkle with the brown sugar and place as close as possible under a preheated broiler for a half-minute or so, or until the sugar bubbles and caramelizes a little. Watch it carefully.

4. Cool and refrigerate. Serve Bourdaloue cold.

❀ Pear Gratin

total calories — 872 • per serving — 145

No matter how busy the working day, this is an easy and savory dessert that can be prepared in very little time. Since it is not a temperamental dish, it can be either served immediately when finished baking or held in the turned-off oven for up to an hour.

Serves 6

6	*pears*	(570)
2	*tablespoons fruit jelly (not jam), preferably apple, quince, or apricot*	(102)
½	*cup dry white wine*	(25)
1	*tablespoon orange liqueur or kirsch*	(12)
½	*cup graham cracker crumbs*	(163)

Preheat oven to 350°.

1. Peel the pears and cut them in half lengthwise. Scoop out the center core and seeds; a grapefruit knife works well for this. Place the fruit cut side down in a baking or pie dish that will hold them snugly.

2. In a small bowl, beat the jelly with a fork or wire whisk until it is fairly smooth. Beat in the wine and liqueur or kirsch and pour the sauce over the pears. Cover the dish and bake for 20 to 30 minutes, depending on the ripeness of the fruit. The pears should be soft but still firm when pierced with a small, sharp knife.

3. Remove the cover, sprinkle about 2 teaspoons of graham cracker crumbs over each pear and the remaining crumbs into the cooking liquid. Return the uncovered dish to the oven for 15 minutes. Carefully baste once or twice, taking care not to wash the crumbs off the pears.

4. Serve directly from the baking dish, spooning over each portion some of the thickened sauce produced by the absorption of the liquid by the crumbs.

❋ Pears Poached in Red Wine

total calories — 1748 • per serving — 219

Normally, at least twice as much sugar is used in making the wine syrup, adding almost 100 calories to each portion. Is it missed? Not at all. The sweeter the sauce is, the more it overpowers the natural sugar of the fresh fruit itself. This is a beautiful balance.

Serves 8

1	quart red wine	(200)
1	cup sugar	(770)
1	small lemon, sliced thin	(15)
½	teaspoon cinnamon	(3)
8	pears, Anjou or Bartlett	(760)

1. Measure into an enameled or tin-lined copper pot the wine, sugar, lemon, and cinnamon. Once it has been brought to a boil, cover and simmer for about 20 minutes.

2. Meanwhile, carefully peel the pears (a swivel-bladed vegetable peeler works fine). Leave the stem intact, but remove a slice from the bottom, so the pears will stand up solidly in the serving dish. As soon as each pear is peeled, rub it with a cut lemon, and drop it in a bowl of clear cold water; this is to prevent discoloration. (If you have selected normal-sized pears, leave them whole, for this is the prettiest presentation; if oversized, cut them in half and remove seeds. If you want to speed up the cooking, or prefer a sliced compote, then cut the fruit into thick sections and remove seeds.)

3. When the wine syrup is ready, place the pears in the boiling liquid, cover, and cook slowly until they can be easily pierced with a knife but are still slightly firm. The pears will continue to soften while cooling afterward in the hot syrup. A whole pear should take about 30 minutes, depending on the ripeness and size of the fruit; halves or slices will take much less time. During the cooking process, turn the pears quite often so they will be evenly colored by the wine syrup. Use two wooden spoons for turning so as not to bruise the fruit.

4. When the pears are done, place them in a dish that can also hold the hot sauce. Boil down the wine syrup to one-half its volume, strain it, and pour over the pears. Cover and cool, then chill well.

❀ Ananas à la Créole
(Pineapple with Rum)
total calories — 287 • per serving — 48

Most times when pineapple is flavored with a liqueur it is kirsch, and indeed there is a definite affinity between the tropical fruit and the cherry-based white alcohol. Another equally good combination is with rum, especially when heated and flambéed as in this recipe. A great diet advantage to using rum this way is that its strong flavor precludes the necessity for much sugar, or any butter. The alcohol calories, of course, burn off in leaping blue flames. This is an extremely easy dessert to put together and it appears to be much more wicked than its 118 calories per serving.

Serves 6

6	*slices fresh pineapple, about ½ inch thick*	*(180)*
2	*tablespoons plus ⅓ cup dark rum*	*(84)*
1½	*teaspoons sugar*	*(23)*

Preheat oven to 375°.

1. Place the pineapple slices in a baking dish that holds them snugly and that can also be taken to the table. Sprinkle ½ teaspoon rum over each slice, turn, and repeat on the other side. Let the pineapple marinate for at least 15 minutes, but not more than an hour.

2. Place the baking dish in the hot oven and bake for 10 minutes. Remove the dish from the oven, turn on the broiler, and while it is heating, sprinkle ¼ teaspoon sugar over each pineapple slice. Then broil for about a minute or two to caramelize the sugar a little. Meanwhile, pour the remaining ⅓ cup dark rum into a small pot or butter melter and place on medium heat to warm through.

3. Take the hot baking dish to the table (or sideboard), pour on the hot rum, and ignite by touching with a match. As the flames dance, ladle the rum over the slices with a long spoon. Depending on the size of the dish, it may be necessary to lift the dish at one side to collect the liquid. When the flames begin to die down, transfer the pineapple to individual warm dishes.

✻ Scalloped Plums

total calories — 681 • per serving — 114

Crushed cornflakes are used in this fruit scallop, because their flavor is less intrusive than many other crumb toppings. The cereal already contains a good deal of sugar, so only the smallest amount of additional sugar is required.

Serves 6

1 pound plums (about 7 or 8), split in half and pits removed	(272)
2 teaspoons sugar	(30)
½ teaspoon cinnamon	(3)
2 cups crushed cornflakes (about 2 ounces)	(220)
½ cup orange juice	(54)
1 tablespoon butter, melted	(102)

Preheat oven to 350°.

1. In a baking dish, place plums in a single layer, cut side down. Stir together in a bowl the sugar, cinnamon, and cornflakes. Sprinkle the mixture over the plums.

2. Add the orange juice by carefully pouring it along the sides, not over the cornflake topping. Sprinkle the melted butter over the topping and place in oven. Bake for about 30 minutes or until the fruit is soft and the topping has browned a little. Serve warm.

✻ Pumpkin Surprise

total calories — 1018 • per serving — 170

The pumpkin does triple duty in this dessert. It is the baking vessel, the serving container, and part of the finished product, too. There always is a look of surprise and delight when the steaming hot pumpkin comes to the table. The first taste doubles the pleasure.

Serves 6

4	to 4½-pound pumpkin, preferably with stem intact	(350)
9	ginger snaps	(261)
1	medium apple, unpeeled, quartered, cored, and sliced thin	(61)
1	medium banana, peeled and sliced	(101)
½	cup juice-packed pineapple tidbits	(48)
2	tablespoons brown sugar	(68)
1	cup orange juice	(110)
1	tablespoon orange liqueur	(12)
¼	teaspoon each cinnamon, nutmeg, ginger	(7)
1	teaspoon oil	——

Preheat oven to 350°.

1. With a strong, sharp knife, cut off a lid from the pumpkin and put it aside. Use a heavy spoon to scrape out the seeds and fibers until the inside of the pumpkin is smooth. Place it on a baking dish or large pie dish, one that can be taken to the dining table.

2. Crumble 3 ginger snaps into the bottom of the pumpkin, then layer in half the apples and half the bananas. Drain the juice from the pineapple into a small bowl and reserve. Place half the pineapple over the bananas. Sprinkle with 1 tablespoon brown sugar. Repeat again with ginger snaps, apples, bananas, pineapple, sugar, and a final layer of ginger snaps and sugar. Do not completely fill the pumpkin shell; leave about ¾ inch at the top.

3. To the reserved pineapple juice, add the orange juice, orange liqueur, cinnamon, nutmeg, and ginger. Beat the juices together and pour over the fruit and ginger snaps; the liquid should be barely visible through the top layer of crumbled ginger snaps. If necessary, add a little more orange juice. Replace the lid on the pumpkin, making certain it fits well; follow the cutting line. Pour the oil onto a paper towel and rub it over the surface of the pumpkin to give it a shine.

4. Place the baking dish in the preheated oven and bake for about 2 hours or until the pumpkin flesh is soft. If the fit of the lid is not tight and too much steam escapes, place a piece of alumi-

num foil over the top. Test by removing the pumpkin lid and inserting a small, sharp knife into the pulp.

5. The baked pumpkin should be served very warm, but not piping hot. Present it at the table as it is, remove the lid for the guests to see the steam rise, and provide two spoons for serving. The fruit and pulp are scooped out together.

❦ Rhubarb Compote

total calories — 480 • per serving — 80

The natural sweetness of apples is used here to reduce the potent amount of sugar usually added to tart rhubarb.

Serves 6

1	pound rhubarb	(62)
3	medium apples	(159)
	1-inch strip orange rind, chopped fine	——
⅓	cup sugar	(230)
¼	cup unsweetened apple juice	(29)
	pinch of nutmeg	——

1. Trim the rhubarb, pulling off any thick fibers, and cut into 1-inch pieces. Peel the apples, cut into quarters, and core. Reserve several strips of the peel. Place the fruit in a mixing bowl, sprinkle on the orange rind and sugar, and mix with your hands to distribute the flavorings. Cover and set aside for 15 minutes.

2. Transfer the fruit to a heavy nonaluminum pot. Pour the apple juice into the bowl and swirl it around to dissolve any residual sugar, then add the juice to the pot, plus the nutmeg. Tuck in the reserved apple peeling, which will help intensify the rosy color of the compote. Place on medium heat and bring the juice to a boil. Reduce the heat, cover, and simmer 7 to 10 minutes, or until the rhubarb and apples are soft. Do not overcook. Remove and discard the apple peels and cool the compote.

❃ Orange-soused Spaghetti Squash

total calories — 772 • *per serving — 129*

Once an exotic item available only in California, spaghetti squash — a strange vegetable indeed — is now marketed across the country. Its egg-smooth exterior gives no hint of the spaghetti-like strands that tumble out of the shell once it is cooked. Since spaghetti squash flavor is much more delicate than other winter squashes, it lends itself most obligingly to the realm of desserts. I am especially partial to cooking it with orange juice, which transforms the pale yellow flesh to a deep pumpkin color. Although the cooked squash can be served as a hot dessert — perhaps with a splash of maple syrup — I find the orange flavor is intensified when the vegetable has been chilled for a few hours. There is an additional surprise when the orange sauce that is passed with it is — hot!

Serves 6

1	3-pound spaghetti squash	(348)
2	cups orange juice	(220)
¾	cup Orange Sauce (page 198)	(204)

1. Rinse and dry the squash and cut in half lengthwise with a large, heavy knife. Use a tablespoon to scoop out and discard the seeds and the fibers. Place the two halves in a large enameled or stainless-steel skillet, cut side down. Pour in the orange juice, which should reach a depth of about 1½ to 2 inches; add more juice or water if necessary. Place on a medium fire and once the juice reaches the boiling point, cover the skillet, reduce the heat to low, and simmer for 20 to 25 minutes, or until the hard shell has softened and the interior flesh pulls into strands when lifted with a fork.

2. Check the level of the cooking liquid from time to time. As the squash cooks it will absorb some of the juice. It is not necessary to add more juice or water as long as at least a ¼-inch level

remains. Cool in the skillet. Transfer the squash to a dish, cut side up, pour into the hollows any liquid remaining in the skillet, cover with plastic wrap, and put in the refrigerator to chill.

3. At serving time, use a fork to pull the cooked flesh of the squash onto a dish. Divide these strands among six dessert bowls, preferably glass. Reheat the Orange Sauce and pass it at the table so that it maintains optimal heat. Each diner spoons about 2 tablespoons of the hot sauce over the cold dessert.

Strawberries in Raspberry Sauce

total calories — 652 • per serving — 109

The French name for this classic fruit dessert is Fraises Cardinale. There is no way of really knowing if the name is for the bird or the ecclesiast. Whichever, it is an elegant duet of berry flavors. This recipe keeps sugar to a minimum, thus allowing the natural fruit perfumes to dominate.

Serves 6

3	*pints fresh strawberries*	*(363)*
1	*tablespoon sugar*	*(48)*
	rind of 1 orange, grated	——
½	*cup orange juice*	*(54)*
1	*tablespoon plus 1 teaspoon orange liqueur*	*(47)*
	5-ounce package frozen raspberries (sweetened)	*(139)*
1	*teaspoon lemon juice*	*(1)*

1. Carefully rinse and hull the strawberries and put them in a shallow bowl. Sprinkle over them the sugar, grated orange rind, orange juice, and 1 tablespoon of orange liqueur. Mix gently, preferably with your hands; cover and refrigerate for 2 hours. Turn the berries a few times during this marinating period.

2. Put the raspberries in the blender and add 1 teaspoon of liqueur and the lemon juice. Blend until you have a purée of the fruit. Strain the sauce to remove the seeds. Chill. (If you have

fresh raspberries available, purée in the blender 1 cup of the berries, plus ¼ cup sugar and the liqueur and lemon juice.)

3. About 15 minutes before serving, remove the strawberries from the marinade, either with a slotted spoon or your hands. (The marinade can be frozen for this or other dessert sauces.) Place the berries in a deep serving bowl, pour the raspberry sauce over them, and mix carefully again.

❀ Fruit Kebabs

total calories — 480 • *per serving — 80*

Use this recipe as a guideline. The fruits listed below can generally be bought the year round, but there is no reason that a few strawberries, cherries, tangerines, pears, grapes, or even watermelon can't be strung along as well. Softer-fleshed fruit should be a little firm, or the pieces will fall apart during the broiling.

Serves 6

MARINADE:

¼	cup dark rum	(47)
1	tablespoon honey	(64)
	juice of 1 lemon	(12)
¼	teaspoon nutmeg	(3)
¼	teaspoon ground ginger	(2)

FRUITS:

½	grapefruit	(40)
1	tart medium-large apple	(84)
1	large banana	(116)
½	cup pineapple chunks, fresh or water-packed	(48)
1	orange	(64)

1. To make the marinade, heat the rum to the boiling point in a small pot and spoon the honey into a shallow dish. Stir the hot rum into the honey and add the lemon juice, nutmeg, and ginger.

Remove sections from the grapefruit half and put them aside. Squeeze the juice from the grapefruit shell into the marinade.

2. Add the grapefruit sections to the marinade, then proceed with the other fruit. Quarter the unpeeled apple, core, and cut into 12 pieces. Cut the banana into 12 pieces and section the orange. Put all the fruit in the marinade and spoon some of the marinade over the pieces. Cover and let stand for 1 hour, basting occasionally.

3. String the fruit on six 6-inch skewers, alternating the variety, but beginning and finishing with apple. Put the completed skewers on a baking dish and baste liberally with the marinade. Place under a preheated broiler, about 6 inches away from the flame. Baste several times during the broiling. The kebabs should be finished in about 10 minutes. For the last 2 or 3 minutes, raise the dish to within 3 inches of the flame to brown parts of the fruit. Serve at once, spooning sauce over each kebab.

❃ Strawberry-Apple Compote

total calories — 576 • per serving — 96

When strawberries are at their peak, apples are not. But even out-of-season berries, which rarely have a full sunny flavor, can turn an everyday apple compote into a very special dessert.

Serves 6

1	pound apples (about 3), McIntosh, York, or Stayman	(245)
	juice of ½ lemon	(6)
¼	cup sugar	(192)
½	cup water	———
1	pint strawberries (or 8 ounces unsweetened frozen)	(121)
1	tablespoon kirsch	(12)

1. Peel and quarter the apples, remove the cores, and cut each section in half lengthwise. Place the apples in a saucepot and sprinkle on the lemon juice, sugar, and water. Put on medium heat, and when the water comes to a boil cover and simmer for 5 minutes.

2. Add the strawberries and kirsch, re-cover and cook 1 minute more. Cool, then chill well.

❀ Fruited Custard

total calories — 433 • per serving — 72
per serving with marshmallow topping — 95

This fresh-fruit medley is baked in a fruit-flavored sauce that eliminates the need for any sugar. Even if the optional marshmallow topping is used, you still have a light and delicious dessert that doesn't add up to 100 calories per serving.

Serves 6

1	*medium apple*	*(53)*
1	*medium pear*	*(95)*
½	*medium banana*	*(51)*
2	*eggs*	*(154)*
2	*teaspoons cornstarch*	*(20)*
¼	*teaspoon ginger*	*(2)*
½	*cup orange juice*	*(54)*
1	*teaspoon orange liqueur*	*(4)*
	Optional: 6 large marshmallows (about 1 oz.)	*(138)*

Preheat oven to 350°.

1. Peel, quarter, core, and slice the apple and the pear thin. Peel the banana and cut into thin slices. Mix all the fruit together in an 8-inch pie dish. Press down the fruit a little to smooth the top surface.

2. Break the eggs into a small bowl, sprinkle on the cornstarch, and beat together well with a fork. Add the ginger, orange juice, and orange liqueur and beat again until thoroughly blended. Pour the liquid over the fruit. If necessary, press down the fruit slices again so that they are just covered by the liquid.

3. If using marshmallows, dip a sharp knife into hot water and slice each marshmallow in half horizontally. Place the cut marshmallows on top of the fruit slices. Put in the oven for about 45

minutes, or until the custard has set and the marshmallows have browned and melted a little. A knife plunged in the center should come out clean. Serve warm or at room temperature. If refrigerated, remove from the refrigerator at least an hour before serving.

❁ Fruit Snowball

total calories — 183 • per serving — 46

This rich-tasting dessert is purity itself. It is nothing more than frozen fresh fruit and a little fruit juice whizzed together. The fruit goes into a food processor in chunks and comes out thick, creamy, and voluminous.

Serves 4

1 cup strawberries, or other seasonal fruit	(55)
1 medium banana	(101)
¼ cup orange (or other fruit) juice	(27)

1. Rinse and hull the berries and place them in a plastic bag or box. Peel the banana, cut it into 1-inch chunks, and immediately roll tightly in plastic wrap. Place the fruit in the freezer to freeze solid.

2. At serving time, place the frozen fruit in the container of a food processor, pour on the juice, and process with the metal blade. At first the fruit will be chopped into small bits, then amalgamated into a creamy pink mass. Serve at once.

❁ Champagne Fruit Cup

total calories — 745 • per serving — 124

Only the champagne and sherbet remain fixed in this recipe. The fruits should change with the season — using canned or frozen fruits with champagne would be like spreading beluga caviar on RyKrisp. This is one flashy way of getting a lot of mileage out of a mere half-bottle of that delightful bubbly wine.

Serves 6

¼ cup strawberries, sliced	*(14)*
¼ cup bananas, diced	*(32)*
¼ cup pineapple, diced	*(21)*
¼ cup peaches, diced	*(18)*
2 tablespoons sugar	*(92)*
1 tablespoon kirsch	*(35)*
1 cup Lemon Sherbet (page 118)	*(206)*
½ bottle champagne, well chilled	*(327)*
Optional: mint sprigs, whole strawberries, or	
crystallized flowers for garnish	

1. Prepare the fruits, sprinkle with the sugar and kirsch, and turn carefully with your hands. Cover and chill for about 3 hours. Chill 6 parfait or wine glasses.

2. At serving time, spoon the fruit into the chilled glasses, pouring over each portion some of the collected juices. Add a small scoop of Lemon Sherbet and top with a garnish, if used.

3. At the table, open the bottle of champagne and pour a little over each fruit cup.

✤ Sauternes

The venerable Grand Véfour restaurant in Paris serves a glass of Sauternes wine after dinner. It is listed on the dessert menu, not the wine card. How right they are. The better the bottle of Sauternes, the richer and more luscious the golden wine. Good French Sauternes can be expensive, so it makes eminently good sense to enjoy it for itself instead of relegating it to its usual role of accompanying a sweet dish. Small glasses of the icy liqueurish wine can be sipped with nothing more than a simple cookie, if that.

Please do not confuse American wines called "dry sauterne" with the imported product. The name itself is a contradiction in terms since true Sauternes is inherently sweet. Although Château d'Yquem is the most famous of the Sauternes, it is also the most expensive, some vintage bottles fetching fifty dollars. Scout around and you can still find good French Sauternes for an eighth that price.

Sauternes is included here with other fruits since it is, after all, nothing but the juice of grapes.

Serves 1

1½	ounces chilled Sauternes	(30)
1	half-bottle serves 8.	

❦ Candied Orange Peel

Candied Orange Peel can decorate many desserts, whether they contain the same fruit or not. The cooked peel adds a pretty, curly note on top of poached pears, crêpes, custards, bananas, and many other compatible sweets. The peel can be candied anytime you are using oranges and have no need for the skins. Once cooked, they keep for weeks in the refrigerator in a tightly covered container.

orange peel
water
sugar
nutmeg

1. With a swivel-bladed vegetable peeler, carefully remove the rind from the oranges, making certain that none of the white underskin is included. Cut the rind into very, very thin juliennes and place in a small, heavy pot.
2. Measure and pour on enough water to cover the peel by ½-inch. For each ½ cup water, sprinkle on 1 tablespoon of sugar and ¼ teaspoon grated nutmeg. Put over moderately high heat and bring to a boil, cover, and simmer for 10 minutes.
3. Remove the cover, reduce the heat to a simmer, and continue cooking until all the water has evaporated and the julienned peel is coated with a light syrup. Stir occasionally at the beginning of the cooking and more often as the water level is

reduced. Cool the candied peel, spoon into a small container, cover tightly, and refrigerate until needed.

✿ Frappés

Halfway between a drink and a dessert lie frappés. In addition to being thick, frothy desserts, they can play many other delicious roles. Think of them as a semiliquid breakfast on a hot summer day, a refreshing late-afternoon sipping potion, or even an incredibly low-calorie lunch. Because of their consistency you will find them remarkably filling; the crushed ice cubes add to the volume and thickness. Furthermore, frappés are ready in a whiz and are completely adaptable to your fruit preferences as well as your refrigerator stock. Part of their secret is in processing the frappé at the last minute, but of course, all ingredients except the fruit and ice could be measured into the container of the blender or food processor, ready to go at the flick of a button. Improvisation is part of the fun of frappés, but keep in mind that to achieve a rich, velvety quality some bulky ingredient must be included; banana is particularly good in this role.

✿ Banana-Carob Frappé
total calories — 156 • per serving — 39

Serves 4

½	medium banana, peeled	(51)
1	cup skimmed milk	(88)
½	teaspoon vanilla	(3)
½	tablespoon carob powder	(14)
4	ice cubes	——

1. Place all ingredients in the container of an electric blender or food processor and process until the mixture is thick and frothy, about 3 minutes. Hold down the top of the container when starting the motor and for about 20 seconds, until the ice

cubes have been crushed a little. Before the ice has been completely crushed it can be heard striking against the container; process until it can no longer be heard. There should be about 3½ cups of frappé.

2. Pour the frappé into tall glasses, preferably chilled; pass long spoons. Serve at once.

❀ Apple-Apricot Frappé

total calories — 194 • per serving — 49

Serves 4

½	cup apricot nectar	(72)
¾	cup skimmed milk	(72)
1	small-to-medium apple, peeled and cut into chunks	(50)
	pinch of cinnamon	——
4	ice cubes	——

Follow directions for Banana-Carob Frappé in the preceding recipe.

❀ Pineapple Frappé

total calories — 184 • per serving — 46

Serves 4

⅔	cup pineapple pieces	(54)
1	cup skimmed milk	(88)
2	teaspoons sugar	(30)
1	teaspoon kirsch	(12)
4	ice cubes	——

Follow directions for Banana-Carob Frappé recipe on the preceding page.

✿ Orange Frappé

total calories — 208 • per serving — 52

Serves 4

1	small orange, peeled and cut into chunks	(45)
1	cup skimmed milk	(88)
¼	cup orange juice	(27)
1	tablespoon sugar	(46)
¼	teaspoon vanilla	(2)
4	ice cubes	——

Follow directions for Banana-Carob Frappé recipe (page 44).

✿ Buttermilk-Fruit Frappé

total calories — 80

This frappé is not quite as thick as others because it uses no whole fruit. Some can be added, if you like, but I find this refreshing drink-dessert perfect as is.

Serves 1

¼	cup buttermilk	(22)
¼	cup fruit nectar — apricot, peach, banana, etc.	(37)
1	teaspoon honey	(21)
	pinch of nutmeg	——
1	ice cube	——

Follow directions for Banana-Carob Frappé recipe (page 44).

❄ Gelatin Desserts
Mousses, Snows, Jellies,
Aspics, Creams

MOLDED DESSERTS deliver a lot of mileage for their calories. They are pretty, brimming with good flavors, light, and blessedly low in calories. In many cases the slimming magic comes from beaten egg whites, which add great volume at minimal caloric expense. Once mixed with well-flavored bases, the frothy whites emerge as shimmering confections that create extra portions for the same amount of sugar.

Unflavored gelatin is another prop in the foundation of low-calorie desserts. Natural juices can be turned into jellies, as in California Sweet. Wines provide an excellent source for aspics in this chapter. Once wine is heated to 180 degrees Fahrenheit, most of the alcohol and calories evaporate, leaving behind only the grape-based flavor and a bit of residual sugar — a true dieter's delight. Pick your wine color — red, white, or rosé — and you will find a recipe to suit.

Although sugar is whittled down throughout this book, molded cream desserts needed further alterations. Heavy cream has given way to evaporated milk, both full-fat and skimmed. Once properly chilled, canned milk whips up to a most impressive mass, providing just the right amount of creaminess to hold fruit purées in suspension.

As with all gelatin preparations, these must be finished at least several hours in advance. But there is no reason the busy cook can't put them together the day before. All in all, gelatin desserts can be counted on for a great many things, except calories.

✾ California Sweet

total calories — 487 • per serving — 81

All the sunshine of California is captured in these shimmering molds of poached oranges caught in orange aspic. The natural goodness of the fruit itself precludes any heavy-handed flavor additions.

Serves 6

2	navel oranges	(128)
2	cups orange juice	(220)
2	tablespoons sugar	(92)
2	tablespoons orange liqueur	(24)
¼	cup water	——
1	tablespoon gelatin	(23)

1. Carefully remove the rind from the oranges with a swivel-bladed vegetable peeler; include none of the white pith. Slice the rind into very thin juliennes. Cut away all the white pith from the oranges, then on a small cutting board or dish slice the oranges into ¼-inch rounds. Place the slices in a small pot and add any juice that collected on the board. Pour in the orange juice, the julienned rind, sugar, and orange liqueur. Bring the juice to the boiling point, cover, reduce the heat, and simmer gently for 30 minutes.

2. Meanwhile, pour the water into a small bowl or cup and sprinkle with the gelatin; put aside to soften. Lift the cooked orange slices and rind out of the juice with a slotted spoon and put them in a sieve suspended over a bowl. Immediately stir the softened gelatin into the hot juice and stir to dissolve it completely; put aside to cool.

3. Add to the orange juice aspic any liquid that has drained from the slices. Measure the juice. There should be 2 cups; if not, add water to fill out the amount. Select 6 individual serving bowls, preferably glass, put them on a tray or baking sheet, and pour half the syrup into the bowls. Place in the refrigerator to set the jelly.

4. Reserve the julienned rind. Cut the orange slices in half,

then into wedge-shaped pieces. Reserve 6 of the largest pieces. Divide the remaining orange wedges among the 6 dishes, spoon on a tablespoon or two of the orange syrup, and return to the refrigerator to set the orange pieces in place. Pour on the remaining syrup and chill until it, too, has set.

5. To serve: Decorate each dish with a reserved orange wedge, pushing the point into the set jelly, then sprinkle with the reserved orange rind juliennes.

❀ Coffee Jelly

total calories — 305 • per serving — 51

A coffee-flavored dessert is always a welcome finish to a meal. If you are concerned about guests who don't drink caffeine, simply use decaffeinated coffee. It will alter the final taste minimally.

Serves 6

3¼ cups water	——
¼ cup Kahlúa, brandy, or rum	(47)
4 tablespoons instant coffee, preferably freeze-dried	(20)
¼ cup sugar	(192)
2 tablespoons plain gelatin	(46)
Optional: ½ cup Whipped Topping (page 203) flavored with ½ teaspoon Grand Marnier	

1. Measure into a pot 3 cups water, the alcohol, coffee, and sugar. Place on heat and bring to a boil. Simmer for a half-minute, uncovered.

2. Meanwhile, pour the remaining ¼ cup water in a small bowl and sprinkle on the gelatin; put aside to let soften. Remove the boiling liquid from the heat and stir in the softened gelatin; continue stirring until dissolved. Cool.

3. Pour the coffee into a dish measuring approximately 8 × 12 × 1 inches; the coffee should not be deeper than ¾ inch. Chill until set.

4. Cut the Coffee Jelly into cubes of about ½ inch and place in individual serving saucers or bowls; glass bowls are the prettiest. If the optional Whipped Topping is used, pass it separately.

❀ Bacchus Oranges

total calories — 754   •   per serving — 94

Though red wine is often used to poach pears, peaches, and even apples, not often is it thought of for oranges. Now Bacchus Oranges will prove there is a treat we've been missing. Here the wine serves first as the poaching liquid, then is turned into an aspic that embraces the fruit sections.

Serves 8

3	cups coarse red wine	(150)
⅓	cup sugar	(230)
½	teaspoon cinnamon	(3)
¼	teaspoon nutmeg	(3)
4	seedless oranges	(256)
1	tablespoon orange liqueur	(12)
½	cup orange juice	(54)
2	tablespoons gelatin	(46)
	Optional: Candied Orange Peel (page 43) for garnish	

1. Pour the wine, sugar, cinnamon, and nutmeg into a non-aluminum pot. Simmer for 5 minutes, uncovered. Meanwhile, remove the skin from the oranges and cut the sections of fruit out from between the membranes. Work over a bowl to collect the dripping juice. Add the oranges and juice to the syrup, turn up the heat, and once the syrup comes to a boil again, remove the pot from the heat, cover, and let stand for 15 to 30 minutes.

2. Lift the orange sections out of the syrup with a slotted spoon and put them into a sieve suspended in a bowl. Add the orange liqueur to the poaching syrup and place on medium heat. Pour the orange juice into a small bowl, sprinkle on the gelatin, and let stand a few minutes to soften. When the wine syrup comes to a boil, remove the pot from the heat and stir in the softened gelatin to dissolve. Cool the syrup.

3. Select a 6-cup ring mold and pour into it just enough of the syrup to film the bottom. Place the mold in the refrigerator to set the wine aspic. Arrange a layer of orange slices over the aspic

and carefully spoon over them just enough wine syrup to barely cover them. Refrigerate again to set the fruit in the aspic. Fill the mold with the remaining orange sections. Add to the aspic syrup any syrup that drained from the oranges. Carefully pour the remaining aspic syrup over the oranges and refrigerate for several hours, or until the aspic is firmly set.

4. To serve: Reverse the mold onto a chilled serving platter and if desired, decorate with the optional Candied Orange Peel sprinkled on top.

✿ Swiss Fruit Ring
(Pears in White Wine Jelly)
total calories — 803 • per serving — 100

Though watches and cheese may be Switzerland's best-known exports, that Alpine country also has important wine and fruit productions. The white wines are particularly agreeable. And as for the fruit — raspberries and pears particularly — they are usually shipped around the world in the form of *eaux-de-vie* (white alcohols), and none come packaged more spectacularly than the whole pear nestled inside a bottle of white pear brandy. Fresh pears and a light white wine are combined in this sparkling Swiss molded dessert, to which bananas are added, not for authenticity, but just as a bit of exotica.

Serves 8

3	cups dry white wine	(150)
⅓	cup sugar	(230)
1	teaspoon vanilla	(6)
½	teaspoon nutmeg	(6)
	orange rind strip about 1 × 2 inches	——
2	pears	(190)
½	cup apple juice	(59)
2	tablespoons gelatin	(46)
1	large banana	(116)

51

1. Measure into a flat skillet the wine, sugar, vanilla, and nutmeg. Add the orange rind, place on the heat, and once the liquid comes to a boil, cover, reduce the heat, and simmer for 5 minutes.

2. Meanwhile, peel the pears, cut into eighths, and core. Add the pears to the syrup, re-cover, simmer for 2 or 3 minutes, then remove from the heat and let stand for 15 minutes without removing the cover.

3. Lift the pear slices out of the syrup with a slotted spoon and put them into a sieve suspended in a bowl. Pour the apple juice into a small bowl or cup and sprinkle on the gelatin; put aside to soften. Return the skillet to the fire and once the syrup reaches the boiling point, remove from the heat and stir in the gelatin. Stir well to completely dissolve the gelatin. Cool the syrup.

4. Select a 6-cup ring mold and pour into it just enough of the syrup to film the bottom. Place the mold in the refrigerator to set the wine aspic.

5. Peel the banana, pull off any fibrous strings, and cut into thin diagonal slices. Arrange a pattern of alternating pear and banana slices over the set aspic. Add to the aspic syrup any wine syrup that drained from the pears and spoon a little over the fruit. Return the mold to the refrigerator to set the fruit in aspic. Add the remaining banana slices to the cool aspic syrup to prevent discoloration.

6. Fill the mold with the remaining pear slices. Lift the banana slices out of the syrup and mix them with the pears. Carefully pour the aspic syrup over the fruit and refrigerate for several hours, or until the aspic is firmly set.

7. To serve: Reverse the mold onto a chilled serving platter.

✿ Rosé Jelly

total calories — 294 or 340 • per serving — 49 or 57

Obviously, this Rosé Jelly can be made the year round, since the main ingredient comes out of the bottle. But perhaps because of its pale rosy color, I find it a particular delight in the summer. Come to think of it, however, because it has so few calories it could easily correct the balance of an otherwise heavy winter meal.

Serves 6

3¼ cups rosé wine	(163)
1 to 2 tablespoons sugar, depending on sweetness of wine	(46 to 92)
¼ teaspoon nutmeg	(3)
3 tablespoons water	——
3 tablespoons kirsch	(36)
2 tablespoons gelatin	(46)
Optional: sliced fruit for garnish	

1. Pour the rosé into an enameled or tin-lined pot; add the sugar and nutmeg and bring to a boil. Reduce the heat and simmer gently, uncovered, for 1 minute. Meanwhile, pour the water in a small bowl and sprinkle the kirsch and gelatin over it; put aside to soften the gelatin. Remove the pot from the fire and immediately stir in the gelatin to dissolve it. Cool.

2. Pour the rosé into a dish measuring approximately 8 × 12 × 1 inches; the liquid should not be deeper than ¾ inch. Chill.

3. Cut the Rosé Jelly into cubes of about ½ inch and place them in individual saucers or bowls; glass bowls are the prettiest. Place the bowl on a saucer and add any optional fruit garnish.

❀ Rosé Jewels

total calories — 415 to 461 • per serving — 35 to 38
with 3 berries — 50 to 53

Rosé Jewels are based on the preceding Rosé Jelly, with one big difference. That single change is the strawberry incorporated into each molded serving, displacing a good deal of jelly and adding a bright red note within the pink. This is one of the prettiest, as well as lightest, desserts your guests can be served. Though a muffin tin is efficient to use because of its compactness in the refrigerator, you may find custard cups are easier to unmold, since they can be handled individually.

Serves 12

3¼	cups rosé wine	*(163)*
1 to 2	tablespoons sugar, depending on sweetness of wine	*(46 to 92)*
¼	teaspoon nutmeg	*(3)*
3	tablespoons water	——
3	tablespoons kirsch	*(36)*
2	tablespoons gelatin	*(46)*
1	pint strawberries, stemmed	*(121)*
12	small parsley sprigs	——

Optional: 12 large leaves — ivy, grape, or similar; 36 strawberries for garnish

1. Follow step 1 in preceding recipe for Rosé Jelly.

2. Place 12 muffin or custard cups on a cookie sheet and fill with the rosé to a depth of about ½ inch. Chill until fairly firm. Meanwhile, fill the stem hole of the berries with the parsley sprigs. Place one parsley-topped strawberry in the center of each cup, parsley end down. Chill until firm. Pour in the remaining rosé to fill the cups. Chill again until firm. If the berries are large and their tips show above the level of the jelly, slice off to the jelly level.

3. To serve: Shine the leaves by rubbing with a little oil. Put a leaf in the center of each plate. Unmold each Rosé Jewel, place on the leaf, and garnish with 3 fresh strawberries. (Other fruits can be substituted — peaches, grapes, cherries, nectarines.)

❀ Apple Snow

total calories — 522 • per serving — 65

Apple Snow has a delicate and frothy appearance from a combination of flecks of applesauce suspended in an apple aspic with beaten egg whites. I like to emphasize its delicateness by not using an overpowering amount of spices. That's a personal preference, however, and minor flavoring adjustments will not affect its ethereal look or calorie count.

Serves 8

2 cups unsweetened apple juice	(234)
2 tablespoons gelatin	(46)
2 tablespoons maple syrup	(100)
1 cup unsweetened applesauce	(100)
½ teaspoon nutmeg	(6)
½ teaspoon cinnamon	(3)
½ teaspoon vanilla	(3)
2 egg whites, room temperature	(30)
pinch of cream of tartar	——

1. Chill a 6-cup ring mold. Pour ½ cup of the apple juice into a small bowl, sprinkle on the gelatin, and put aside to soften. Meanwhile, pour the remaining 1½ cups of apple juice into a small pot, add the maple syrup, and put on a medium fire to simmer for 3 minutes. Remove the pot from the heat and stir in the softened gelatin until dissolved.

2. Spoon the applesauce into a mixing bowl and add the nutmeg, cinnamon, and vanilla. Stir to mix the flavorings, then pour in the apple juice and mix well. Put the bowl aside to cool until the mixture thickens a little.

3. Beat the egg whites in a bowl with the cream of tartar. When they are firm, scoop about one-third of the beaten whites onto the applesauce mixture and blend the two together quite thoroughly. Add the remaining beaten whites and fold them in carefully; do not overmix or the whites will break down. Immediately pour the mixture into the chilled mold and refrigerate until the snow has set, about 3 hours.

4. Unmold the Apple Snow on a chilled dish and use two large spoons for serving.

❀ Apricot Whip

total calories — 954 • per serving — 119

With all the extra calories in dried apricots as compared with the fresh fruit, they have a very concentrated flavor. This allows stretching the packaged apricots to the maximum number of servings while still retaining a rich taste. Furthermore, less sugar is needed, because dried apricots are quite sweet. Here is a perfect example of carefully evaluating what the calories bring with them and using it judiciously.

Serves 8

½	pound dried apricots	*(590)*
1¾	cups water	——
¼	cup sugar	*(192)*
½	cup orange juice	*(54)*
1	tablespoon orange liqueur	*(12)*
2	tablespoons gelatin	*(46)*
4	egg whites, room temperature	*(60)*
	pinch of cream of tartar	——

1. Rinse the apricots and place them in a saucepan. Bring 1¼ cups water to a boil and pour over the apricots. Cover and let stand for 2 hours. Put the covered pan over moderate heat and cook gently until the fruit is tender, about 30 minutes. Cool slightly, then pass the fruit and liquid through a food mill. The mill is preferable to a blender because it is certain to remove any tough pieces of skin.

2. Return the apricot purée to the pot, add the sugar, orange juice, and liqueur, and put on low heat. Meanwhile, soak the gelatin in ½ cup cold water and, once it is softened, add the gelatin to the hot purée. Remove from heat and stir the gelatin until it is dissolved. Keep the mixture warm while you beat the egg whites, but do not allow the purée to boil.

3. Add a pinch of cream of tartar to the egg whites and beat until they are very stiff. Mix one-quarter of the beaten whites into the apricot mixture and fold in well. Lightly spoon the apricot mixture over the remaining beaten whites and fold in gently. Pour into a deep serving or soufflé dish and chill until firm.

4. To serve: Carefully cut around the whip, dip the bottom of the mold into warm water, reverse the mold onto a chilled serving platter, and give a sharp shake to release it. Cut into the whip with two large spoons.

❦ Citron en Neige

(Lemon Snow)

total calories — 804 • *per serving — 80*
with garnish — 90

A minimal amount of gelatin, and a small prayer, keep this snow-white dessert together. It actually quivers when brought to the table. One could easily add extra gelatin, but a firmer texture would, to my mind, destroy the pristine purity of the snow. If by some unhappy chance the dessert collapses when unmolded — which shouldn't happen — simply heap it into individual dessert dishes.

Serves 10

¾ cup sugar	(577)
2¼ cups water	——
2 tablespoons gelatin	(46)
1 tablespoon grated lemon rind	——
1 cup lemon juice	(61)
8 egg whites, room temperature	(120)
pinch of cream of tartar	——
Optional: rind from 4 lemons, 1 cup water,	
2 tablespoons sugar, to make garnish	(92)

1. Put sugar and 1¾ cups of water in a pot, stir over heat until the sugar dissolves, and boil for 2 minutes. Meanwhile, soften the gelatin in ½ cup water and add this to the hot syrup, stirring completely to dissolve the gelatin. Add the grated lemon rind and lemon juice. Keep on very low heat or on a flame-deflector pad.

2. Add the cream of tartar to the egg whites and whip until they are very stiff. At this point you will need either an electric beater or someone to help you. While continuing to beat the whites, pour on the hot lemon syrup. Beat for a full minute.

3. Place the mixing bowl in a larger bowl or a pot filled with ice and a little water. With a rubber spatula mix the snow to help cool it quickly. Keep the bowl in the ice water bath until the snow becomes quite thick, mixing occasionally to thoroughly blend the syrup with the beaten whites.

4. Select a 10-cup soufflé dish or other mold. Place a moistened

round of waxed paper in the bottom of the mold and pour in the lemon mixture. Tap the mold firmly on the table to settle the snow well into the dish. Smooth the top and refrigerate until set, about 3 to 4 hours.

5. To serve: Slide a hot knife around the mold, place a chilled serving platter over the mold, and invert; give a sharp shake to unmold the snow. Remove the wax paper and decorate with optional garnish, if desired.

Garnish: Cut the lemon rind into thin juliennes and put in a small pot with 1 cup of water and 2 tablespoons of sugar. Boil uncovered until almost all of the water has evaporated and the rind is lightly caramelized. Scrape into a small bowl, cover, and refrigerate until needed. This caramelized rind keeps well under refrigeration.

❀ Brandy Ring

total calories — 498 • per serving — 83

This molded dessert is more scented than flavored. Though its delicacy makes it a perfect foil for fresh fruit, more than likely you will want to enjoy it straight. As in all alcohol cooking, the better the bottle, the better the end result, but great sipping cognac would be overdoing it.

Serves 6

¾	cup skimmed milk	(72)
1	tablespoon gelatin	(23)
1	egg yolk	(62)
¼	cup sugar	(192)
¼	cup brandy	(47)
1	teaspoon vanilla	(6)
½	cup evaporated skimmed milk	(96)
½	teaspoon lemon juice	———
	Optional: fresh strawberries, sliced fruit, or Chocolate Sauce (page 196) for garnish	

1. Pour ¼ cup skimmed milk into a small cup, sprinkle on the gelatin, and put aside to soften. Into a heavy nonaluminum pot,

pour the remaining ½ cup skimmed milk and bring it to the boiling point.

2. Meanwhile, beat the egg yolk and sugar together in a mixing bowl until light and frothy. Pour the hot milk over the egg-sugar mixture while whisking vigorously. Return the hot milk mixture to the pot, place on a low fire, and cook while whisking constantly until the sauce will coat a spoon. Once the egg yolk has been added to the hot milk, the sauce must not be allowed to boil. Stir in the brandy and vanilla and cook another half-minute while whisking. Remove the pot from the heat and stir in the gelatin. Cool the sauce, then refrigerate until it thickens to a syrupy consistency. Beat with the whisk from time to time.

3. While the sauce is thickening, pour the evaporated skimmed milk into a mixing bowl and place in the freezer along with the beaters from the electric beater. The milk should be icy just about the time the sauce has thickened. Add the lemon juice to the chilled milk and beat at high speed until the milk triples in volume and thickens.

4. Beat the thickened brandy sauce with the wire whisk, add about one-third of the whipped milk, and blend in thoroughly with the whisk. Add the remaining whipped milk and carefully and lightly fold it into the mixture, using a rubber spatula.

5. Very lightly oil a 4- or 5-cup ring mold and spoon in the brandy mixture. Refrigerate for at least 3 hours, or until the mixture has set. Unmold onto a serving dish.

6. The molded dessert can be served plain, or the center can be filled with strawberries or other fruit; alternatively, Chocolate Sauce can be spooned over the Brandy Ring.

✽ Gossamer Caramel

total calories — 533   •   per serving — 67

To get as much impact as possible from the sugar used in this whipped sweet, it is turned into a caramel before being poured over beaten egg whites, producing a variation on Italian meringue. You will notice that the gelatin is brought to the boiling point, a procedure usually avoided, since high heat breaks down the protein in gelatin and destroys its jelling properties. The reason for treating it this way here is to produce an attractive nut-brown coating on top of the unmolded dessert.

Serves 8

1	tablespoon gelatin	*(23)*
9	tablespoons water	——
½	cup sugar	*(385)*
7	egg whites, room temperature	*(105)*
	pinch of cream of tartar	——
½	teaspoon orange liqueur	*(2)*
1	tablespoon vanilla	*(18)*
	Optional: Creamy Dessert Sauce (page 195)	

1. In a very small pot, soften the gelatin in 4 tablespoons of water, then put on slow heat to gradually bring it to the boiling point. At the same time, in another pot (preferably a heavy one), boil together the sugar and 3 tablespoons of water. Do not stir, but rotate the pot from time to time as the sugar is cooked over high heat until it caramelizes and turns dark brown.

2. While the sugar is caramelizing and the gelatin is dissolving, add the cream of tartar to the egg whites and begin beating. When the egg whites are quite firm, pour in the hot gelatin and continue beating. As soon as the caramel has become dark brown, pour it over the egg whites, beating constantly. Return the caramel pot to the fire, add 2 tablespoons of water and the orange liqueur, and bring to a boil to dissolve the residual caramel. Pour this flavored water over the egg whites while beating; finally, add the vanilla and beat at high speed for about a half-minute.

3. Lightly oil a 10-cup mold of any shape — a round-bottomed mixing bowl is especially well suited. Scoop in the caramel mixture and tap the mold on the table a few times to settle the mixture well into the container. Smooth the top of the caramel mixture and refrigerate overnight, or for at least 3 hours.

4. Run a hot flexible knife around the dessert, first reaching halfway down the sides of the bowl, then a second time, reaching all the way to the bottom. Dip the bottom of the bowl in hot water for a few seconds, then place a chilled serving dish over the bowl and invert. If the optional sauce is used, spoon a little of it around the bottom of the dessert and pass the rest in a sauceboat.

✻ Pineapple Bavarian

total calories — 1003 • per serving — 125

When it comes to Bavarians, looks can be misleading. They appear to be a light dessert but actually are loaded with calories, mostly from cream, egg yolks, and sugar. This version tempers the calories, not the flavor.

Serves 8

1	lb.-4 oz. can crushed unsweetened pineapple	(350)
¼	cup water	——
2	tablespoons gelatin	(46)
2	tablespoons kirsch	(24)
⅓	cup sugar	(230)
1	cup evaporated milk	(345)
2	tablespoons lemon juice	(8)
	Optional: fresh or crystallized mint leaves or pineapple wedges for garnish	

1. Place a sieve over a bowl and pour in the pineapple to drain. There should be approximately 1 cup of juice and a scant 2 cups of fruit. Pour the water into a small bowl, sprinkle on the gelatin, and put aside to soften. Pour the juice into a pot, add the kirsch, and place on the heat to bring just to the boiling point. Remove the pot from the heat and immediately add the gelatin, stirring until it is completely dissolved. Add the sugar and set aside to cool slightly.

2. Put the crushed pineapple in a large mixing bowl and pour the juice over it. Chill until it is almost syrupy.

3. Meanwhile, pour the milk into a large bowl and place in the freezer until ice crystals begin to form; also chill the beaters. When ready to whip the milk, add the lemon juice, then beat on high speed until the milk triples in volume and is quite firm.

4. Take about one-third of the whipped milk and thoroughly fold it into the chilled pineapple; then delicately fold in the remainder. Place the bowl in the refrigerator until the Bavarian begins to set; carefully stir the mixture once or twice to keep the pineapple pieces in suspension. Lightly oil a 6-cup mold and

spoon the Bavarian into it, tapping the mold on the table a few times to settle the cream well into the container. A ring mold is especially suitable.

5. To serve: Unmold the Pineapple Bavarian onto a chilled plate and, if desired, decorate with the optional garnishes.

❦ Chocolate Sponge

total calories — 450 • per serving — 75
with garnish — 85

With just a few ingredients that are generally on hand, the busy cook can put together this good-to-look-at and good-to-eat dessert. Even without the addition of butter it has a lavish flavor and beautiful texture, thanks to the least possible dilution of the cocoa taste.

Serves 6

½	cup water	——
1	tablespoon gelatin	(23)
¼	cup cocoa	(56)
¼	cup sugar	(192)
	pinch of salt	——
1	teaspoon vanilla	(6)
1	teaspoon orange liqueur	(4)
2	egg yolks	(124)
	pinch of cream of tartar	——
3	egg whites, room temperature	(45)
	Optional: 12 strawberries for garnish	

1. Chill a 4-cup mold — either a fluted container, soufflé dish, or ring mold. Pour ¼ cup water into a small bowl or cup and sprinkle on the gelatin. Put aside to soften.

2. Measure the cocoa, sugar, and salt into a heavy pot and stir to combine them. Pour in the remaining ¼ cup of water and stir again to dissolve the cocoa and sugar. Place the pot on medium

heat and stir until the mixture cooks to the boiling point. Remove the pot from the heat, immediately add the vanilla, orange liqueur, and softened gelatin and stir until it dissolves completely. Cool the mixture for 2 minutes.

3. Place the egg yolks in a large mixing bowl and beat lightly, then slowly pour in the hot mixture while beating vigorously with a wire whisk. Put this chocolate base aside to cool and thicken slightly.

4. Add the cream of tartar to the egg whites and beat them until thick and firm. Scoop about one-third of the whites onto the chocolate sauce and mix the two together very well to lighten the thick mixture. Add the remaining beaten whites and fold them in carefully and thoroughly. Spoon the sponge into the chilled mold and place in the refrigerator until set.

5. To serve: Unmold the Chocolate Sponge onto a chilled serving dish. If you would like a color contrast, place a few of the optional strawberries around the dark sponge.

❀ Potted Pumpkin

total calories — 516 • per serving — 86

For this year-round dessert, pumpkin comes out of its usual pie shell and into any handy mold, preferably one with a rounded bottom. Even an ordinary mixing bowl can be used. Although cooked, fresh pumpkin pulp can be substituted, this recipe uses canned pumpkin so that it can be enjoyed right around the calendar. Besides, the pumpkin-selling season has been getting shorter and shorter. At one time you could count on buying it most fall and winter months, but no more. Now fresh pumpkin is widely available for Halloween, Thanksgiving, and a bit at Christmas, but in between those holidays one cannot count on it. I suppose we must chalk it up as another victim of streamlined produce marketing.

Serves 6

1	*cup unsweetened pumpkin*	*(81)*
½	*cup apple juice*	*(59)*
2	*tablespoons maple syrup*	*(100)*
2	*tablespoons brown sugar*	*(68)*
½	*teaspoon cinnamon*	*(3)*
½	*teaspoon nutmeg*	*(6)*
½	*teaspoon ginger*	*(3)*
1	*tablespoon gelatin*	*(23)*
½	*cup evaporated milk*	*(172)*
1	*teaspoon lemon juice*	*(1)*
	Optional: 1 cup Ginger Sauce (page 198)	

1. Stir together in a saucepot the pumpkin, ¼ cup apple juice, maple syrup, brown sugar, cinnamon, nutmeg, and ginger. Put over medium fire, heat to the bubbling stage, and allow to cook for about a half-minute.

2. Meanwhile, pour the remaining ¼ cup apple juice in a small bowl or cup and sprinkle on the gelatin; set aside to soften. Remove the saucepot from the fire and immediately stir in the gelatin to dissolve it completely. Scrape the pumpkin mixture into a large mixing bowl and put aside to cool and thicken slightly.

3. While the mixture is cooling, pour the evaporated milk into a mixing bowl and place in the freezer along with the beaters. At the same time, chill in the refrigerator a 4- or 5-cup nonstick mold or other vessel, preferably with a round base. A very light wiping with vegetable or mineral oil will facilitate the unmolding if an ordinary utensil is used.

4. When the pumpkin mixture has thickened a little, whip the milk. Add the lemon juice to the icy milk and beat at high speed until the liquid becomes thick and creamy and triples in volume. Spoon about one-third of the whipped milk into the pumpkin bowl and mix the two thoroughly. Add the rest of the whipped milk and delicately fold it into the lightened pumpkin batter. Spoon the dessert into the chilled mold and refrigerate until set, about 3 hours.

5. To serve: Unmold the Potted Pumpkin onto a serving platter and use two large spoons for cutting into it. If the optional Ginger Sauce is used, pass it separately.

❀ Maple Mold

total calories — 664 • per serving — 83

Small wonder maple syrup is so popular. Not only does it do an emphatic sweetening job, but it also adds its own sparkling flavor. This double-duty performance is capitalized on here.

Serves 8

½ cup water	——
2 tablespoons gelatin	(46)
¾ cup evaporated skimmed milk	(144)
½ cup pure maple syrup	(400)
2 teaspoons rum	(8)
1 teaspoon vanilla	(6)
4 egg whites, room temperature	(60)
pinch of cream of tartar	——
Optional: Rum Sauce (page 199)	

1. Pour the water into a small bowl or cup and sprinkle on the gelatin and put aside to soften. Pour the evaporated skimmed milk and maple syrup into a heavy pot, add the rum, and bring to the boiling point. Remove the pot from the fire and immediately add the gelatin, stirring to dissolve it completely, then add the vanilla. Pour the hot liquid into a mixing bowl to cool, then chill until it is syrupy.

2. Put the egg whites in a bowl, add the cream of tartar, and beat the whites until they are firm. Using the same beater, whip the maple syrup until fluffy. Take about one-third of the whites and thoroughly fold them into the whipped syrup. Delicately fold in the remaining whites. Lightly oil a 6-cup mold and scoop in the dessert; tap the mold on the table a few times to settle the mixture well into the container. Chill until firm.

3. Unmold the dessert onto a chilled serving platter. If desired, pass the optional Rum Sauce separately.

❦ Cocoa Mold

total calories — 490 • per serving — 98

This chocolate dessert is composed of just a handful of ordinary kitchen cupboard items. It could almost be considered an emergency dessert, except that it doesn't have the dreary look or taste of one.

Serves 5

¼ cup water	——
1 tablespoon gelatin	(23)
¾ cup evaporated skimmed milk	(144)
⅓ cup sugar	(230)
3 tablespoons cocoa	(42)
1 teaspoon vanilla	(6)
3 egg whites, room temperature	(45)
pinch of cream of tartar	——
Optional: Rum Sauce (page 199)	

1. Pour the water into a small bowl or cup and sprinkle on the gelatin; put aside to soften. Put the milk in a heavy pot and slowly bring it to the boiling point. Meanwhile, mix the sugar and cocoa together in a bowl, then pour in the scalded milk while beating with a wire whisk. Add the gelatin at once and stir until it has dissolved. Add the vanilla and mix well. Cool the mixture, then chill until it is syrupy.

2. Put the egg whites in a bowl, add the cream of tartar, and beat until the whites are firm. Using the same beater, whip the cocoa sauce until fluffy. Scoop about one-third of the whites onto the whipped sauce and thoroughly fold them in. Delicately fold in the remaining whites. Lightly oil a 4-cup mold and spoon the dessert into it; tap the mold on the table a few times to settle the mixture well into the container. Chill until firm.

3. Unmold the dessert onto a chilled serving platter. If the optional sauce is used, pass it separately.

❦ Banana Cream

total calories — 379 • per serving — 63
with garnish — 70

There is so little gelatin in this dessert — ½ tablespoon in almost
6 cups of mousse — that Banana Cream should not be considered
a molded dessert at all. The tiny bit of gelatin is included only as
insurance for staying power. I often ignore it totally, but only
when the cream will not be held for more than three or four
hours.

Serves 6

1	teaspoon kirsch	(4)
1½	tablespoons lemon juice	(6)
2	medium bananas	(202)
7	tablespoons water	——
½	tablespoon gelatin	(12)
2½	tablespoons sugar	(110)
3	egg whites, room temperature	(45)
	pinch of cream of tartar	——
	Optional: 3 or 4 thin banana slices for garnish	

1. Pour the kirsch and lemon juice into the blender container.
Peel the bananas, pulling off any fibrous strings. Start the blender,
break off chunks of banana, and feed them into the container.
Process until the bananas are a smooth purée; there should be
about 1 cup. Pour the purée into a small pot, scraping in every
bit that might remain in the bottom of the container.

2. Pour 1 tablespoon water into a small bowl or cup, sprinkle
on the gelatin, and put aside to soften. Put the sugar and 4 tablespoons water in another small pot. Place the pot on high heat to
boil for at least 3 minutes while beating the egg whites.

3. Place the egg whites in a large mixing bowl and add the
cream of tartar. Immediately begin beating with an electric beater
and when the whites are quite firm, pour on the boiling syrup
while continuing to beat at high speed. Pour the syrup quickly or
some of it will harden as it cools, resulting in hard, candied sugar

bits. Add 2 tablespoons of water to the syrup pot and return to the heat to dissolve any syrup clinging to the bottom and sides of the pot; boil for at least a half-minute. While waiting for the dissolving syrup to be ready, continue beating the whites at medium speed. Meanwhile, place the pot containing the banana purée over medium heat.

4. Swirl the syrup pot and pour the dissolved syrup over the whites while beating. At this point the whites should be very thick and glossy and look almost like heavy whipped cream.

5. Once the banana purée reaches the bubbling stage, remove the pot from the heat and stir in the softened gelatin. Stir to dissolve the gelatin thoroughly, then pour the purée over the whites while beating on slow speed.

6. Spoon the Banana Cream into a 6-cup soufflé dish or other serving bowl. Individual dessert bowls can also be used. Chill well.

7. At serving time, garnish with a few banana slices, if desired, cutting them thin and on the diagonal to produce elongated slices.

❈ Blueberry Cream

total calories — 340 • per serving — 57

Though Blueberry Cream is best made when the fruit is fresh, this dessert is too good to limit to that brief period. Frozen berries can be substituted outside the growing season. There is a good mathematical reason for serving this mousse often: The strong flavor of the berry means a little goes a long way, resulting in even fewer calories than in the other fruit creams. If the dessert will not be held for more than three hours, the gelatin can be omitted.

Serves 6

1	*cup blueberries, fresh, or unsweetened frozen, thawed*	(90)
¼	*cup plus 1 tablespoon water*	——
¼	*cup sugar*	(192)
1	*tablespoon lemon juice*	(4)

1	tablespoon kirsch	(12)
½	tablespoon gelatin	(12)
2	egg whites, room temperature	(30)
	pinch of cream of tartar	——

1. Put the blueberries in a pot and add ¼ cup water, the sugar, and lemon juice. Bring the water to a boil, cover, reduce the heat, and simmer for 10 minutes. With a slotted spoon, lift the berries out of the syrup and put them in a blender. Purée the fruit, then scrape it into a small pot.

2. Pour the kirsch and 1 tablespoon of water into a small bowl or cup, sprinkle on the gelatin, and let it soften. Put the cooking syrup on medium heat. In a large bowl, beat together the egg whites and cream of tartar until the whites are firm. At this point, turn up the heat under the berry syrup and once a full rolling boil is reached, pour the juice over the beaten whites and continue beating at high speed for at least 3 minutes.

3. Meanwhile, put the berry purée on medium heat and once it begins to bubble, remove from the fire and stir in the softened gelatin to dissolve it completely. Immediately pour the purée over the beaten whites and beat at medium speed for another 2 or 3 minutes to cool the mixture.

4. Spoon the mousse into a 6-cup soufflé dish or other serving bowl and refrigerate for at least 3 hours.

❀ Orange-Rum Cream

total calories — 796 • per serving — 100

Rum and orange go as well together as rum and Coke — even better to my mind. The velvety smoothness of this dessert cream gives no hint of its true calorie count.

Serves 8

2	cups skimmed milk	*(176)*
2	tablespoons gelatin	*(46)*
¼	cup sugar	*(192)*
1	tablespoon rum	*(12)*
2	eggs, separated, room temperature	*(154)*
1½	cups orange juice	*(164)*
	rind 2 oranges, grated	——
1	tablespoon lemon juice	*(4)*
	pinch of cream of tartar	——
	Garnish: 8 fresh orange sections and 8 mint sprigs	*(48)*

1. Pour ½ cup milk into a small bowl and sprinkle in the gelatin; put aside to soften. Meanwhile, put the remaining 1½ cups milk, sugar, and rum in a heavy nonaluminum pot and place on a heat-deflector pad over medium heat. When the milk comes almost to the boiling point, remove from the heat and stir in the softened gelatin.

2. Place the egg yolks in a mixing bowl and beat lightly. Pour in the hot milk, whisking vigorously as you do. Pour the milk and yolks back into the pot and return to the heat (still over the heat-deflector pad) and cook, stirring constantly until the mixture thickens and coats a spoon, about 5 minutes. Do not allow the sauce to boil. Remove from the heat and stir in the orange juice, orange rind, and lemon juice.

3. Beat the egg whites and cream of tartar together in a large mixing bowl. When the whites are stiff, carefully pour in about one-third of the hot orange sauce and fold delicately with a rubber spatula. Repeat with the remaining orange sauce, adding half at a time. Ladle the dessert cream into 8 deep custard dishes and refrigerate until set.

4. To serve: Cut the membranes away from the 8 orange slices and place 1 in the center of each dish. If available, a small mint sprig is an attractive addition.

❀ Pear Cream

total calories — 454 • per serving — 76

This is a real fool-the-eye dessert. It looks like a bowl of wicked whipped cream. At the first taste, though, eyes light up at the sparkling freshness of the pear flavor. Without the garnish of pear slices the initial mystery is deeper still. If the dessert will not be held for more than three hours, the gelatin can be omitted.

Serves 6

4	tablespoons sugar	*(192)*
2	tablespoons kirsch	*(24)*
1	teaspoon vanilla	*(6)*
½	cup plus 1 tablespoon water	——
2	pears (¾ to 1 lb.)	*(190)*
½	tablespoon gelatin	*(12)*
2	egg whites, room temperature	*(30)*
	pinch of cream of tartar	——

1. Pour into a flat skillet 3 tablespoons of sugar, 1 tablespoon of kirsch, the vanilla, and ½ cup water. Cover and place on high heat while peeling the pears. Cut the pears into quarters and core the sections. Add the pears to the syrup, cover, and poach for 5 to 7 minutes, depending on the ripeness of the fruit. The pears should be soft when pierced with a small, sharp knife. Use a slotted spoon to remove the pears from the syrup and place them in the blender. If a garnish for the dessert is desired, trim off 3 or 4 thin pear slices and reserve. Purée the pears, then pour them into a small pot and place on low heat.

2. Add 1 tablespoon of the cooking syrup to the purée and pour the rest of the syrup into a small pot. Add 1 tablespoon of sugar to the syrup and put on medium heat to simmer. In a small bowl or cup, pour 1 tablespoon of water and 1 tablespoon of kirsch and sprinkle with the gelatin; put aside to soften.

3. Place the egg whites in a large mixing bowl and add the cream of tartar. Turn up the heat under the syrup. Immediately begin beating the egg whites with an electric beater and when they are quite firm, pour on the boiling syrup while continuing

to beat at high speed. Pour the syrup quickly or some of it will harden as it cools, resulting in hard, candied sugar bits. At this point, the whites should be very thick and glossy and look almost like heavy whipped cream.

4. Turn up the heat under the pear purée and once it reaches the bubbling stage, remove the pot from the fire and stir in the softened gelatin. Stir to dissolve the gelatin thoroughly, then pour the purée over the whites while beating on slow speed.

5. Spoon the Pear Cream into a 6-cup soufflé dish or other serving bowl. Individual dessert bowls can also be used. Chill well. At serving time, garnish with the reserved pear slices.

❀ Strawberry Cream

total calories — 364 • per serving — 73

By using the Italian meringue principle of adding hot syrup to beaten egg whites, a mere two whites become the creamy foundation for a whole bowlful of this prettily pink strawberry dessert. If the dessert will not be held for more than three hours, the gelatin can be omitted.

Serves 5

	10-oz. package frozen sweetened strawberries, defrosted	(310)
1	tablespoon water	——
2	teaspoons orange liqueur	(8)
½	tablespoon gelatin	(12)
1	tablespoon lemon juice	(4)
2	egg whites, room temperature	(30)
	pinch of cream of tartar	——

1. Select a 3-cup soufflé dish and fit it with a wax paper collar. (If using a mold that will not accommodate a collar, select one that holds 4 to 5 cups.)

2. Place the strawberries in a sieve suspended over a bowl. Pour the water and orange liqueur into a small bowl, sprinkle on the gelatin and let it soften. Scrape the drained strawberry pulp into

72

a blender, add the lemon juice, and process until puréed. Pour the purée into a small pot and place on medium heat. When it is hot, scrape in the softened gelatin, remove the pot from the heat, and stir to dissolve the gelatin.

3. Pour the strained strawberry juice into a small pot and place on medium heat to simmer for 3 or 4 minutes. Meanwhile, put the egg whites in a large mixing bowl, add the cream of tartar, and beat until firm. At this point, turn up the heat under the strawberry juice and once a full rolling boil is reached, pour the juice over the beaten whites while continuing to beat at high speed. Beat for at least 3 minutes; the whites should become thick and smooth, resembling a pink whipped cream.

4. Reheat the strawberry purée gently — do not allow it to boil — and pour it over the beaten whites while beating. Beat at medium speed for another 3 or 4 minutes to cool the mixture. Spoon the strawberry cream into the dish and refrigerate for at least 3 hours.

5. Carefully remove the collar from the soufflé dish and place the dish on a round platter. Serve with 2 large spoons.

Note: Because a minimal amount of gelatin is used, Strawberry Cream is best made the day it is to be served. It will hold perfectly well for one day, but begins to soften after that.

❄ Plum Foolish

total calories — 549 • per serving — 92

This is an American cousin to the English dessert called Fool. Traditionally, it is served in individual dishes, since its fluffiness makes less of an impression in a large presentation. Be prepared for a deep rosy color that might be mistaken for something out of a dye bottle. Here is proof positive that Mother Nature can be as flamboyant as the chemists.

Serves 6

1 *pound plums (about 7 or 8)*	*(272)*
½ *cup water*	———
3 *tablespoons sugar*	*(138)*
1½ *tablespoons kirsch*	*(18)*
1 *tablespoon gelatin*	*(23)*
½ *cup evaporated skimmed milk*	*(96)*
2 *teaspoons lemon juice*	*(2)*

1. Rinse the plums and put them in a small pot that will hold them snugly. Pour in ¼ cup water, cover, and bring to a boil. Cook until soft, about 5 minutes. Uncover the pot and let the fruit cool.

2. When the plums are cool enough to handle, slip off the skins, pull the fruit away from the seed, and put the pulp into an electric blender or food processor. Leave the dark purple cooking juices in the pot. Purée the fruit; there should be about 1¼ cups of purée. Return it to the pot and add the sugar and kirsch. Slowly bring it to a simmering point.

3. Meanwhile, pour the remaining ¼ cup water into a small cup and sprinkle on the gelatin. When it is softened, add it to the hot fruit, remove the pot from the heat, and stir until the gelatin is dissolved. Cool, then chill until the mixture becomes syrupy.

4. During this time, pour the milk into a mixing bowl and place in the freezer until ice crystals form. Also chill the beaters. When the milk is ready to whip, add the lemon juice and beat at high speed until it triples in volume. Using the same beaters, beat the plum purée, then scrape the whipped milk over the fruit and delicately blend the two together with a rubber spatula. The dark purple purée will tone down to a deep rose color. Place the bowl in the freezer for 15 minutes to set the small amount of gelatin quickly.

5. Have ready 6 individual chilled serving dishes. Spoon the slightly set mixture into the dishes and refrigerate until serving time. With a fork, lightly fluff each portion of Plum Foolish.

❀ Puddings and Custards

CUSTARDS AND PUDDINGS are deservedly popular at the
American table. They are refreshing desserts that appear in
a rainbow of flavors. You will find, among the recipes that follow,
apricot, orange, apple, honey, maple, chocolate, coffee, banana,
lemon, and even white wine. With such good assistance from nature, richness is not needed. Skimmed milk replaces cream, cocoa
is usually used instead of oil-rich chocolate, and egg yolks are cut
back and replaced by a little cornstarch. A whole tablespoon of
the starch adds only 29 calories against 62 for one yolk. What
counts is the texture and taste of the finished dish, not how you
got there. I believe you will find these desserts lead straight to
palate pleasure without an overload of calories.

Another caloric-control device used in this book is smallish —
not small — portions. Most people tend to eat everything put in
front of them, hungry or not. We learned our lessons well at
mother's table. Since more is often eaten than is really wanted,
why tempt thickened waistlines? Custards can be baked in small
cups, pretty *pots de crème*, or the easily purchased foil muffin
baking cups. Individual servings always are attractive, because
they are a complete unit unto themselves.

✿ Chocolate Pudding

total calories — 678 • per serving — 68

Choco-holics have a rough time of it when trying to watch weight. Ounce for dusky ounce, they can count on 150 calories in pure chocolate. And who stops at a mere ounce? In cooking, on the other hand, cocoa can be substituted to reduce the calorie count drastically. Chocolate and cocoa are almost identical twins emerging from the cacao bean. Fat is the only difference between them, and since it is removed from cocoa, calories plummet. This is one way to pamper your chocolate freaks while helping them watch their waistlines.

Serves 10

⅓ cup sugar	(230)
2 tablespoons cornstarch	(58)
¼ teaspoon salt	——
⅓ cup cocoa	(70)
2 cups skimmed milk	(176)
1 egg	(77)
1 teaspoon rum	(4)
2 teaspoons vanilla	(12)
½ tablespoon butter	(51)
10 2½-inch paper-lined foil muffin cups, custard cups, or pots de crème	

1. With a whisk, mix the sugar, cornstarch, and salt together in a heavy 1-quart nonaluminum pot. Stir well to coat the cornstarch particles with sugar, which will help prevent lumps from forming in the pudding. Add the cocoa and stir again.

2. Add the milk slowly while stirring with the whisk, keeping the sauce as smooth as possible. Put the pot on medium heat and bring to the bubbly and thick stage. Cook for 2 or 3 minutes longer to remove any starchy taste. Stir almost constantly during this period to keep the pudding from burning.

3. Beat the egg and rum together in a small mixing bowl. Pour about a cupful of the hot sauce over the egg while beating vigorously. Scrape the egg and sauce back into the pot and continue

cooking for another minute, stirring constantly. Remove the pot from the heat, add the vanilla and butter, and stir until it has completely melted. Place a piece of plastic wrap directly on top of the pudding to prevent a skin from forming. Cool. Arrange the serving cups on a tray or baking dish and spoon the chocolate pudding into them. Chill well.

❀ White Wine Pudding

total calories — 523 • per serving — 87

I first came across white wine pudding in the heart of Germany's wine-growing region. After tramping through vineyards all morning, the hearty luncheon and cool pudding were devoured by the group. A simple local (Rheinpfalz) wine was used. Like most German white wines, this one, too, was fruity with a hint of sweetness. Any of the imported Liebfraumilchs is suitable, or California's Chenin Blanc.

Serves 6

3	tablespoons sugar	(138)
3	tablespoons cornstarch	(87)
½	cup skimmed milk	(44)
2	cups sweet white wine, Chenin Blanc or Liebfraumilch	(100)
2	eggs	(154)

1. Select a heavy nonaluminum pot (tin-lined copper or enameled cast iron are perfect), measure directly into it the sugar and cornstarch, and mix them together. With a wire whisk, stir in the milk and wine. Place the pot over very low heat and slowly bring the liquid to the simmering point. Whisk often, but once it begins to simmer, beat constantly until the sauce thickens. (If there is any danger of cooking too rapidly, place the pot on a heat-deflector pad.)

2. Put the eggs in a mixing bowl. Slowly pour the sauce over the eggs while beating vigorously with the whisk. Return the sauce to the pot and cook for 1 minute more, again whisking constantly. Do not allow it to boil.

3. Spoon the pudding into six individual dessert dishes (glass is prettiest). Cover immediately with plastic wrap to prevent a crust from forming. Cool, then chill.

4. To serve: The pale yellow pudding needs no decoration, but if preferred, it can be garnished with a single crystallized violet (or similar) in the center.

❀ Blanc Mange
(Cornstarch Pudding)

The traditional Blanc Mange is a mildly flavored vanilla pudding. Its popularity depends on a very generous proportion of sugar, plus rich milk and cream. Furthermore, to compound the calorie problem, it is usually offered with a sweet syrup. In the three Blanc Mange puddings given below, sugar is pared to a minimum while taste appeal is maintained through additional flavorings. Since each has a distinctive character of its own, smothering sauces would be completely out of place.

❀ Orange Blanc Mange
(Orange Cornstarch Pudding)

total calories — 532 • per serving — 106

Serves 5

2 tablespoons sugar	(92)
3 tablespoons cornstarch	(87)
¼ teaspoon salt	——
½ cup skimmed milk	(44)
½ teaspoon lemon juice	——
2 cups orange juice	(220)
1 tablespoon orange liqueur	(12)
1 egg	(77)
Optional: crystallized violets or *Candied Orange Peel* (page 43) for garnish	

1. Select a heavy nonaluminum pot and measure directly into it the sugar, cornstarch, and salt; mix together. With a wire whisk, stir in the milk, lemon juice, orange juice, and orange liqueur. Place the pot on a heat-deflector pad over medium heat. Slowly bring the liquid to a simmer, whisking constantly, until it thickens.

2. Have a beaten egg ready in a mixing bowl. Slowly pour the sauce over the egg, beating vigorously with the whisk. Scrape in all the hot sauce. Return the sauce to the pot and cook for 1 minute more, again whisking constantly. Do not allow it to boil.

3. Spoon the Blanc Mange into a 4-cup serving dish, or into 5 individual dessert dishes. Cover with plastic wrap to prevent a crust from forming. Cool, then chill well. At serving time, it can be decorated with the optional garnish: a single crystallized violet or a few strands of Candied Orange Peel.

❃ Apricot Blanc Mange
(Apricot Cornstarch Pudding)

total calories — 598   •   per serving — 120

Serves 5

2 tablespoons sugar	(92)
3 tablespoons cornstarch	(87)
¼ teaspoon salt	——
½ cup skimmed milk	(44)
½ teaspoon lemon juice	——
2 cups apricot nectar	(286)
1 tablespoon orange liqueur	(12)
1 egg	(77)
Optional: crystallized violets for garnish	

1. Select a heavy nonaluminum pot and measure directly into it the sugar, cornstarch, and salt; mix together. With a wire whisk, stir in the milk, lemon juice, apricot nectar, and orange liqueur. Place the pot on a heat-deflector pad over medium heat. Slowly bring the liquid to a simmer, whisking constantly, until it thickens.

2. Have a beaten egg ready in a mixing bowl. Slowly pour the sauce over the egg, beating vigorously with the whisk. Scrape in all the sauce. Return the sauce to the pot and cook for 1 minute more, again whisking constantly. Do not allow it to boil.

3. Spoon the Blanc Mange into a 4-cup serving dish, or into individual dessert dishes. Cover with plastic wrap to prevent a crust from forming. Cool, then chill well. At serving time, it can be decorated very sparingly with the crystallized violets — only 1 in the center of the individual servings, or just 3 or 4 centered in the larger bowl.

❀ Chocolate Blanc Mange
Chocolate Cornstarch Pudding)
total calories — 650 • per serving — 130

Though this Chocolate Blanc Mange weighs in with a few extra calories more than the fruit juice puddings, it is far leaner than the usual versions that call for super-rich chocolate.

Serves 5

¼	cup sugar	(192)
¼	cup cocoa	(56)
¼	teaspoon salt	——
3	tablespoons cornstarch	(87)
2½	cups skimmed milk	(220)
1	teaspoon vanilla	(6)
1	tablespoon rum	(12)
1	egg	(77)

1. Select a heavy nonaluminum pot and measure directly into it the sugar, cocoa, and salt. Stir with a wire whisk to blend them together thoroughly. Add the cornstarch and mix again. Stir in the milk, vanilla, and rum. Place the pot on a heat-deflector pad over medium heat. Slowly bring the liquid to a simmer, whisking constantly, until it thickens. Be sure to reach all corners of the pot while whisking, because cocoa thickens quickly.

2. Have a beaten egg ready in a mixing bowl. Slowly pour the

sauce over the egg, beating vigorously with the whisk. With a rubber spatula, scrape out every bit of the cocoa sauce into the egg bowl. Return the egg and sauce to the pot and cook for 1 minute more, again whisking constantly. Do not allow it to boil.

3. Spoon the Blanc Mange into a 4-cup serving dish, or into 5 individual dessert dishes. Cover with plastic wrap to prevent a crust from forming. Cool, then chill well.

❄ Banana Tapioca

total calories — 377 • per serving — 63

Unfair as it may be, plain tapioca carries forever a boarding-school image. Fruits and judicious flavorings can go a long way toward correcting that childhood prejudice. Here fresh banana not only lends its tropical aroma, but stretches the basic recipe to provide more servings, consequently fewer calories.

Serves 6

1	cup banana nectar or orange juice	(110)
2½	tablespoons quick-cooking tapioca	(75)
1	tablespoon sugar	(46)
½	teaspoon almond extract	(4)
1	tablespoon lemon juice	(4)
1	large banana	(116)
¼	cup skimmed milk	(22)

1. Pour the nectar or juice into a heavy enameled pot, stir in the tapioca and sugar, and set aside for about 5 minutes. Place the pot on medium heat and cook until the mixture thickens, about 5 minutes. Stir constantly while the tapioca is cooking. When done, the individual grains will have expanded and turned translucent and not be readily identifiable. Cool for a few minutes, stir in the almond extract, and put aside to cool completely.

2. Process together in the blender the lemon juice, banana, and skimmed milk. There should be about 1¼ cups of purée. Stir the purée into the tapioca and beat with a wire whisk until fluffy. Chill well before serving.

❀ Fluffy Chocolate Tapioca

total calories — 527 • per serving — 88

This dusky tapioca variation is an especially popular one. The addition of beaten egg whites makes it particularly light and airy.

Serves 6

2	*tablespoons cocoa*	*(28)*
3	*tablespoons sugar*	*(138)*
	pinch of salt	——
2	*cups skimmed milk*	*(176)*
2½	*tablespoons quick-cooking tapioca*	*(75)*
1	*tablespoon vanilla*	*(18)*
1	*egg, plus 1 egg white, room temperature*	*(92)*
	pinch of cream of tartar	——

1. Stir together in a heavy enameled pot the cocoa, sugar, and salt. Slowly pour in the milk while stirring. Sprinkle on the tapioca and put aside for 5 minutes.

2. Place the pot over medium heat and cook until the mixture thickens and the tapioca grains expand and become translucent, about 5 minutes; stir often. Reduce the heat, cover the pot, and cook another minute without stirring. Separate the whole egg, add the white to the extra white, and place the yolk in a mixing bowl. Beat the yolk lightly and slowly pour over it the hot tapioca while beating with a wire whisk. Return the hot sauce to the pot and cook another half-minute, stirring constantly. Do not allow the mixture to boil. Cool the tapioca for 5 minutes, add the vanilla, then cool completely.

3. Add the cream of tartar to the 2 egg whites and beat until soft peaks are formed. Fold the beaten whites into the cool tapioca, one-half at a time. Chill the tapioca until ready to serve.

❅ Pineapple Tapioca

total calories — 540 • per serving — 68

Here is a rather sunny version of tapioca with flecks of pineapple dotting the fluffy white pudding. A surprising contrast can be added with a light sprinkling of cinnamon or nutmeg over the top, at no calorie expense.

Serves 8

1	cup crushed unsweetened pineapple	(140)
1¾	cups skimmed milk	(160)
	pinch of salt	——
3	tablespoons quick-cooking tapioca	(90)
1	egg, plus 1 egg white, room temperature	(92)
1	tablespoon kirsch	(12)
	pinch of cream of tartar	——
1	tablespoon sugar	(46)
	Optional: cinnamon or nutmeg	

1. Pour the pineapple and its juice into a sieve suspended over a bowl. Measure the liquid; there should be about ¼ cup. Add enough milk to the juice to make 2 cups and pour into a heavy saucepot. Sprinkle on the salt and tapioca and put aside for 5 minutes. Place the pot on medium heat and cook until the sauce thickens and the tapioca grains become translucent; stir occasionally. This cooking should take about 5 minutes. Cover the pot and cook another minute without stirring.

2. Meanwhile, separate the whole egg, adding the white to the extra white. Place the yolk in a mixing bowl, add the kirsch, and beat lightly, then pour in the hot sauce while beating with a wire whisk. Return the sauce to the pot and cook another half-minute, stirring constantly. Cool the sauce.

3. Add the cream of tartar to the egg whites and beat until soft peaks are formed. Sprinkle on the sugar and continue beating until the whites become firm. Fold the beaten whites into the tapioca, one-half at a time; do not overmix. Allow the mixture to cool completely; it will thicken as it cools. Stir in the crushed pineapple and put the bowl in the refrigerator to chill thoroughly.

While it is chilling, mix the tapioca several times to keep the fruit suspended in the pudding.

4. If desired, dust the Pineapple Tapioca with cinnamon or nutmeg just before serving.

❀ Lemon Tapioca

total calories — 596 • per serving — 99

This is not only a lemon-flavored dessert, it is *whole* lemon-flavored. As one who loves the tang of lemon, I've long been intrigued with the idea of boiling lemon, puréeing it — rind and all — and adding to basic recipes. It didn't work with rice, but it does with tapioca, emphatically so. The puréed citrus adds almost no color to the tapioca, so the crisp flavor comes as quite a surprise. This would be an excellent filling for Crêpes (page 188). In this case, increase the milk to 4 cups and spoon the sauce into the crêpes while still warm.

Serves 6

2	lemons	(40)
3½	cups skimmed milk	(308)
4	tablespoons quick-cooking tapioca	(120)
2	tablespoons honey	(128)

1. Drop the whole lemons in boiling water. Adjust the heat to keep the water at a fast simmer; this will keep the lemons rotating in the water. No need to cover. Cook about 30 minutes, or until the skins look slightly translucent. Cool.

2. Pour the milk into an enameled saucepot, sprinkle on the tapioca, and put aside for 5 minutes. Add the honey and place on a heat-deflector pad over medium heat. Cook while stirring until tapioca thickens.

3. Cut off the ends of the lemons and any ink-stamp marks. Cut the lemons into chunks and remove seeds. Place the cut-up pieces in the blender container and process a little. Pour in the hot tapioca and process until the lemons are completely puréed. Pour into 6 individual serving dishes or parfait glasses, or a 4-cup dish. Cool, then chill well.

❀ Apple Flan

total calories — 999 • per serving — 167

The sugar power in this flan is maximal. Instead of using it just to sweeten the applesauce, it is turned into a caramel that not only sweetens, but also strongly flavors the fruit. You get double the impact for the same number of calories.

Serves 6

½	cup sugar	(385)
2	tablespoons water	——
3	eggs	(231)
1	tablespoon cornstarch	(29)
1	teaspoon vanilla	(6)
¼	teaspoon cinnamon	(2)
1	tablespoon honey	(64)
1½	cups skimmed milk	(132)
1½	cups unsweetened applesauce	(150)

Preheat oven to 300°.

1. Select a 6-cup ovenproof mold, preferably a ring mold with tubular center. Prepare the caramel to line the mold by boiling together the sugar and water in a small, heavy pot. Keep the heat moderate and do not stir the syrup, but swirl the pot from time to time. Keep an eye on the syrup because it can turn from light brown to burnt in seconds. It will take 3 or 4 minutes to reach this stage. When it is a dark nutty color, immediately pour the caramel into the mold and quickly rotate the mold to spread the caramel coating over all surfaces. Use pot holders when handling the mold, because the caramel will be very hot. Put aside to cool and harden the caramel.

2. Break the eggs into a medium-sized mixing bowl and beat until light and fluffy. Sprinkle on the cornstarch and beat well to distribute the starch thoroughly. Add vanilla, cinnamon, and honey and beat again. Stir in the milk, and finally the applesauce. Carefully ladle the flan batter into the caramel-lined mold. Put the mold in a pan containing water that will reach one-third to one-half the depth of the mold. Place in the preheated oven and

bake for about 45 minutes, or until a knife plunged in the center comes out clean. Cool completely, but do not refrigerate at this point.

3. Unmold the flan only after it has cooled. Place a serving dish over the top of the mold and invert the two together. There will be some liquid caramel, so make certain the dish is large enough to contain it. Chill until serving time.

4. To serve: Cut into the baked flan with two large spoons; a little of the liquid caramel sauce can be spooned over each portion.

✸ Cup-of-Chocolate

total calories — 864 • per serving — 86

It may seem like a complete contradiction, but by using pure chocolate in this recipe many, many calories are saved. And because no other enrichments or thickening agents need be added — just a few flavorings and skimmed milk — the full, satisfying taste and texture come from the chocolate itself. But a little bit of good chocolate goes a long way, as this recipe proves. The scant half-cup portions are a perfect finale to a memorable meal.

Serves 10

1½	cups skimmed milk	(132)
2	teaspoons instant coffee, preferably freeze-dried	(2)
1	teaspoon rum	(4)
1	teaspoon vanilla	(6)
5	ounces semisweet chocolate	(720)
10	2½-inch foil baking cups, custard cups, or pots de crème	

1. Pour into a pot the milk, instant coffee, rum, and vanilla, place on medium heat, and bring to the boiling point.

2. Meanwhile, break or cut the chocolate into small chunks and place in the blender. Process to break up the chocolate into still smaller pieces. When the milk comes to the boiling point, pour it into the blender, cover, and let stand about 1 minute. Process until the mixture becomes smooth.

3. Arrange the serving cups on a baking sheet or tray and pour into them the chocolate liquid. Refrigerate until set, which may take as long as 5 hours. (Because no butter or egg is added, it takes longer for the small amount of chocolate to set the liquid.)

4. Place each Cup-of-Chocolate on a saucer along with a teaspoon.

❀ Tofu Gratin

total calories — 637 • per serving — 127

Of late, the near-miraculous nutritional properties of soy beans have been heralded as the dining salvation of a hungry world. It is protein-potent, low in saturated fat, cholesterol-free, rich in minerals and vitamins, and contains few calories. All of these admirable qualities hold true when soy beans are processed into pressed bean curd, sold as tofu. Because it is quite bland in its natural state, it makes a healthful, nonintrusive base for combining with other ingredients and flavorings. In the final dish all the goodness of the tofu is there, but subtly so.

Serves 5

8 ounces tofu	(142)
¾ cup cold cooked white rice	(119)
⅔ cup evaporated skimmed milk	(128)
1 egg	(77)
2 tablespoons honey	(128)
¼ teaspoon ground coriander	(2)
⅛ teaspoon cinnamon	——
2 tablespoons graham cracker crumbs	(41)

Preheat oven to 350°.

1. Place the tofu in a mixing bowl and mash quite thoroughly. Stir in the rice, evaporated skimmed milk, egg, honey, coriander, and cinnamon. Beat well to blend all the ingredients.

2. Lightly oil a 4-cup baking or pie dish. Spoon the mixture into the dish and sprinkle with the graham cracker crumbs. Place in the oven for about 25 minutes, or until a small knife

plunged in the center comes out clean. Put under the broiler for about a half-minute to brown the crumbs. Serve warm.

❀ Unbaked Tofu Custard

per serving — 82 • with wheat germ — 86

The preceding recipe for Tofu Gratin cites the wondrous nutritional properties of tofu (bean curd cake). Here is another way to capitalize on all it has to offer. I find that apricot nectar is the best of the fruit juices when used this way, its rich flavor subduing the slight tanginess of tofu. A half-cup portion is perfect as a light dessert. As a low-calorie lunch it puts packaged fruit-flavored yogurts to shame. A whole cup of Tofu Custard (which is quite filling) would take only 164 points from your daily calorie count, versus 250 to 270 for the yogurts. Since the custard is so easy to prepare — all in the blender — quantities are given for a single serving as well as for six.

Serves 1

2	ounces tofu	(36)
¼	cup apricot nectar	(36)
½	teaspoon sugar	(8)
¼	teaspoon vanilla	(2)
	pinch of nutmeg	⸺
	Optional: ½ teaspoon toasted wheat germ	(4)

Serves 6

12	ounces tofu
1½	cups apricot nectar
1	tablespoon sugar
1	teaspoon vanilla
¼	teaspoon nutmeg
	Optional: 1 tablespoon toasted wheat germ

Place all ingredients, except the wheat germ, in the blender and process until thick and custardlike in consistency. Pour into individual custard cups and chill. If desired, sprinkle with the wheat germ just before serving.

88

✿ Custards

Most custards depend on the richness of egg yolks, milk, cream, and sugar to produce the thick, smooth desserts known in one form or another around the world. By substituting flavorings full of character, plus a hint of cornstarch, almost half the usual number of calories has been whittled away in these recipes. For a crafty sleight-of-hand serving dish, instead of regular custard cups, 2½-inch foil muffin cups are used. One full muffin cup holds about one-third less than the standard 6-ounce baking cup. Even though less custard is being served, it is a satisfying amount and looks like a complete portion because the cup is filled.

✿ Chocolate Custard

total calories — 282   •   per serving — 56

Serves 5

1	cup skimmed milk	(88)
½	teaspoon powdered coffee, preferably freeze-dried	——
1	egg	(77)
	pinch of salt	——
1	teaspoon vanilla	(6)
½	teaspoon cornstarch	(5)
1	tablespoon cocoa	(14)
2	tablespoons sugar	(92)
5	2½-inch diameter paper-lined foil muffin cups	

Preheat oven to 325°.

1. Pour the milk and the powdered coffee in a small, heavy pot and place on heat to bring to the boiling point. Meanwhile, in a mixing bowl beat the egg with a whisk until foamy. Add the salt, vanilla, and cornstarch and beat again until smooth. Sprinkle on the cocoa and sugar and beat until the mixture is smooth once again. Gradually pour the milk in while beating vigorously.

2. Arrange 5 paper-lined foil muffin cups on a baking dish. Use either a ladle or a pitcher to pour the custard liquid into the cups. Carefully pour hot water into the baking dish to reach a level

halfway up the muffin cups. Place in the preheated oven and bake for about 45 minutes, or until a knife plunged in the center comes out clean.

3. Lift the cups out of the water, cool, then chill very well.

❧ Honey Custard

total calories — 278 • per serving — 56

Serves 5

1	*cup skimmed milk*	*(88)*
1	*egg*	*(77)*
½	*teaspoon cornstarch*	*(5)*
	pinch of salt	——
1½	*tablespoons honey*	*(96)*
2	*teaspoons vanilla*	*(12)*
5	*2½-inch diameter paper-lined foil muffin cups*	

Preheat oven to 325°.

1. Scald the milk. With a wire whisk, beat the egg in a mixing bowl until foamy. Add the cornstarch and salt and beat again until smooth. Measure in the honey and vanilla and blend together thoroughly. Gradually pour the hot milk in while beating vigorously with the whisk.

2. Arrange 5 paper-lined foil muffin cups on a baking dish. Use either a ladle or a pitcher to pour the custard liquid into the cups. Carefully pour hot water into the baking dish to reach a level halfway up the muffin cups. Place in the preheated oven and bake for about 50 minutes, or until a knife plunged in the center comes out clean.

3. Lift the custard cups out of the water, cool, then chill very well.

❊ Coffee Custard

total calories — 279 • per serving — 56

Serves 5

1 cup skimmed milk	(88)
1 tablespoon instant coffee, preferably freeze-dried	(5)
1 tablespoon rum	(12)
2 tablespoons sugar	(92)
1 egg	(77)
½ teaspoon cornstarch	(5)
pinch of salt	———
5 2½-inch diameter paper-lined foil muffin cups	

Preheat oven to 325°.

1. Pour the skimmed milk into a small, heavy pot and add the instant coffee, rum, and sugar. Place on heat and bring just to the boiling point.

2. With a whisk, beat the egg in a mixing bowl until foamy. Add the cornstarch and salt and beat again until smooth. Gradually pour the hot coffee-milk in while beating vigorously.

3. Arrange 5 paper-lined foil muffin cups on a baking dish. Use either a ladle or a pitcher to pour the custard liquid into the cups. Gradually pour hot water into the baking dish to reach a level halfway up the muffin cups. Place in the preheated oven and bake for about 50 minutes, or until a knife plunged in the center comes out clean.

4. Lift the custard cups out of the water, cool, then chill very well.

❀ Maple Custard

total calories — 261 • per serving — 52

Serves 5

1	cup skimmed milk	(88)
1	tablespoon brown sugar	(34)
1	teaspoon dark rum	(4)
1	egg	(77)
½	teaspoon cornstarch	(5)
	pinch of salt	————
½	teaspoon maple extract	(3)
1	tablespoon pure maple syrup	(50)
5	2½-inch diameter paper-lined foil muffin cups	

Preheat oven to 325°.

1. Pour the milk into a pot, add the brown sugar and rum, and scald.

2. With a whisk, beat the egg in a mixing bowl until foamy. Add the cornstarch and salt and beat again until smooth. Measure in the maple extract and syrup and blend together thoroughly. Gradually pour the hot milk in while beating vigorously with the whisk.

3. Arrange 5 paper-lined foil muffin cups on a baking dish. Use either a ladle or a pitcher to pour the custard liquid into the cups. Carefully pour hot water into the baking dish to reach a level halfway up the muffin cups. Place in the preheated oven and bake for about 50 minutes, or until a knife plunged in the center comes out clean.

4. Lift custard cups out of the water, cool, then chill very well.

❀ Soufflés and Omelets

ALL THE DRAMA that comes in a towering soufflé is pure gravy for calorie counters. The benefit starts with the French root of the name — *souffler*, which means to blow. What the hot dessert contains, then, is a little sauce base blown up by a lot of air that, as we know, doesn't do diets any harm. The Italian meringue principle is employed for several of these superlight soufflés. By beating hot sauces or syrups into beaten whites, more puffing power is guaranteed.

Omelets are often overlooked as a diet dessert, because they seem so rich. When properly made, and holding low-calorie fillings, they are well within bounds, as the following recipes demonstrate. Usually you need nothing more than a few ingredients found in every refrigerator and cupboard. The fun comes in the mixing and matching.

❀ Soufflé au Grand Marnier

total calories — 333 • per serving — 83

Grand Marnier Soufflé is one of the most popular of all soufflés. In fact, it might be neck-and-neck with chocolate. Those great desserts remind me of one of the more spectacular dinners I attended in Paris. An achingly rich chocolate soufflé was served.

It was delicious. Fine, I thought, I won't have to take seconds when it comes again. But next came an orange soufflé! And who could pass that up? I've since thought how nice they would have been together. After all, Candied Orange Peel is coated in dark chocolate for a popular candy.

This delectably light soufflé is made with absolutely no fat, except for traces in the evaporated skimmed milk. The basic sauce contains no egg yolk, butter, or flour. The calorie count difference is 83 per serving for this recipe, as compared to about 265 for most. Come to think of it, one could also serve a Chocolate Soufflé (next recipe) to make that glamorous duet and still offer fewer calories than a single portion of traditional soufflés.

I am often asked if it is necessary to use Grand Marnier, which has become quite expensive. I think so. Its cognac base gives great strength to the orange-flavored liqueur. But since this recipe also uses orange rind and orange juice, a less-expensive alcohol will not detract too much.

Serves 4

For mold: 1 teaspoon soft butter and 2 teaspoons sugar		*(64)*
1	*tablespoon cornstarch*	*(29)*
2	*tablespoons sugar*	*(92)*
	pinch of salt	——
½	*teaspoon grated orange rind*	——
⅓	*cup evaporated skimmed milk*	*(64)*
3	*tablespoons orange juice*	*(21)*
1½	*tablespoons Grand Marnier*	*(18)*
3	*egg whites, room temperature*	*(45)*
	pinch of cream of tartar	——
	Optional, but recommended: several strands of	
	Candied Orange Peel (page 43) for garnish	

Preheat oven to 425°.

1. Butter a 4- or 5-cup soufflé dish, sprinkle in 2 teaspoons of sugar, and rotate the dish to coat it with the sugar. Put aside. Have a large mixing bowl ready.

2. In a heavy saucepot, stir together the cornstarch, remaining 2 tablespoons of sugar, and salt. Add the orange rind and mix again. Slowly stir in the evaporated skimmed milk, orange juice, and Grand Marnier. Place the saucepot over medium heat and

cook until the sauce thickens; stir constantly. Do not overcook the sauce; it should be about as thick as warm tapioca. Scrape the hot sauce into the large mixing bowl.

3. Immediately begin beating the egg whites with the cream of tartar. When the egg whites are firm, add one-third of them to the orange sauce and fold in thoroughly. Add the remaining beaten whites and fold them in delicately. It is important to work quickly while the sauce is still hot.

4. Scrape the soufflé mixture into the prepared mold. Smooth the top surface and with your finger remove about ¼ inch of batter from around the edge of the dish; this will insure a straight-rising crown. If desired, decorate the center with the optional Candied Orange Peel. Place in the hot oven, reduce the temperature to 375°, and bake for 15 to 20 minutes, or until the puffed top has browned a little and has a slight crack in it. Serve at once.

�֍ Chocolate Soufflé

total calories — 646 • per serving — 81

As in the preceding Soufflé au Grand Marnier, no fats are used for this chocolate version. To maintain the lightness of the dessert and to keep the calories low, cocoa is the basis for the flavoring, but the result is still very much chocolate.

Serves 8

For mold: 1½ teaspoons soft butter and 1 tablespoon sugar		(97)
2	tablespoons cornstarch	(58)
¼	cup cocoa	(56)
	pinch of salt	——
1	teaspoon instant coffee	(1)
3	tablespoons sugar	(138)
1	cup evaporated skimmed milk	(192)
1½	teaspoons vanilla	(9)
1	teaspoon orange liqueur	(4)
6	egg whites, room temperature	(90)
½	teaspoon cream of tartar	(1)

95

Preheat oven to 425°.

1. Butter an 8-cup soufflé dish, sprinkle in 1 tablespoon of sugar, and rotate the dish to coat it with sugar. Put aside. Have a large mixing bowl ready.

2. In a heavy saucepot, stir together the cornstarch, cocoa, salt, instant coffee, and remaining 3 tablespoons of sugar. Slowly stir in the evaporated skimmed milk, vanilla, and orange liqueur. Place the saucepot over medium heat and cook until the sauce thickens; stir constantly. Scrape the hot sauce into the large mixing bowl.

3. Immediately begin beating the egg whites with the cream of tartar. When the egg whites are firm, add one-third of them to the cocoa sauce and fold in thoroughly. Add the remaining beaten whites and fold them in delicately. It is important to work quickly while the sauce is still hot.

4. Scrape the soufflé mixture into the prepared mold. Smooth the top surface and with your finger remove about ¼ inch of batter from around the edge of the dish; this will insure a straight-rising crown.

5. Place in the hot oven, reduce the temperature to 375°, and bake for 15 to 20 minutes, or until the puffed top has darkened a little and has a slight crack in it. Serve at once.

❁ Strawberry Soufflé

total calories — 541 • per serving — 90

Though not quite as strong in flavor, frozen unsweetened strawberries can be used when fresh are not available. They should be thawed before being puréed with their juices.

Serves 6

For mold: 1 teaspoon soft butter and 2 teaspoons sugar	*(64)*
1 *pint strawberries*	*(121)*
1 *teaspoon lemon juice*	*(1)*
1 *teaspoon orange liqueur*	*(4)*
6 *tablespoons sugar*	*(276)*
5 *egg whites, room temperature*	*(75)*

pinch of cream of tartar
Optional: chilled Strawberry Sauce (page 196)

Preheat oven to 375°.

1. Butter an 8-cup soufflé dish. Sprinkle in the sugar and rotate to cover all the greased surfaces.

2. Place the strawberries in the container of a food processor or blender and purée; there will be about 1 cup of purée. Pour the purée into a heavy saucepot, scraping in all of it from the container. Add the lemon juice, orange liqueur, and sugar. Place on medium heat and stir for a half-minute or so, or until the sugar is dissolved. Keep the purée simmering while beating the egg whites.

3. Put the egg whites in a large mixing bowl, add the cream of tartar, and beat the whites until they are very firm. Pour in the hot purée while continuing to beat at high speed. The volume of the beaten whites will expand considerably once the hot sauce is beaten in. Scrape in every bit of purée from the pot and beat again just enough to incorporate the sauce.

4. Spoon the soufflé batter into the prepared mold. Level off the top and with your thumb remove a rim of batter about ¼ inch wide around the edge of the dish. This will help insure a straight-rising crown. Place in the preheated oven and bake for 20 minutes, or until the top is puffed and lightly browned. Serve at once.

❀ Banana Soufflé

total calories — 579 • per serving — 97

Serves 6

For mold: 1 teaspoon soft butter and 2 teaspoons sugar		*(64)*
2	*medium ripe bananas*	*(202)*
2	*teaspoons kirsch*	*(8)*
⅓	*cup sugar*	*(230)*
1½	*tablespoons water*	——
5	*egg whites, room temperature*	*(75)*
¼	*teaspoon cream of tartar*	——

Preheat oven to 425°.

1. Butter an 8-cup soufflé dish. Sprinkle in the sugar and rotate to cover all the greased surfaces.

2. Break the bananas into chunks and purée in the blender or food processor. There should be between 1 and 1¼ cups of purée. Scrape it into a large mixing bowl and stir in the kirsch.

3. Put the sugar and water in a small, heavy saucepot and simmer briskly until it reaches the soft-ball stage (230°). Do not stir the sugar, but swirl once or twice by holding the pot handle and rotating.

4. Once the sugar begins to boil, beat the egg whites with the cream of tartar until they are quite firm. Pour in the hot sugar syrup while beating at high speed until the whites become very thick and glossy. Pour the syrup in quickly, or you risk its hardening as it cools.

5. Add about one-third of the beaten whites to the banana purée and fold in quite thoroughly. Scrape the rest of the beaten whites over the purée and fold in delicately, just enough to blend the two.

6. Spoon the soufflé batter into the prepared mold. Level off the top and with your thumb remove a rim of batter about ¼ inch wide around the edge of the dish. This will help insure a straight-rising crown. Place in the preheated oven and immediately reduce the heat to 375°. Bake about 20 minutes, or until a skewer plunged into it near the edge comes out clean. Serve at once.

✿ Fruit Jelly Soufflé

total calories — 274 • per serving — 69

This soufflé can be made with any number of fruit flavorings. It is based on jelly that is melted and added to beaten egg whites. No other sugar is added to the sauce. It is important to begin with a good jelly, one with a pronounced fruit flavor. A home-made product would be ideal.

Serves 4

For mold: 1 teaspoon soft butter and 2 teaspoons sugar (64)

 2 *tablespoons fruit jelly (not jam) — plum, strawberry,*
   peach, raspberry, apricot, etc. (102)

 1 *teaspoon kirsch* (4)

 ¼ *cup unsweetened apple juice* (30)

 3 *egg whites, room temperature* (45)
   pinch of cream of tartar ———

 1 *tablespoon cornstarch* (29)

Preheat oven to 425°.

1. Butter a 4-cup soufflé dish. Sprinkle in the sugar and rotate to coat the greased surface.

2. Put the jelly, kirsch, and apple juice in a small pot and place on medium heat to boil and melt the jelly. Reduce the heat to low and keep the sauce simmering.

3. Immediately begin beating the egg whites and cream of tartar in a large mixing bowl. When the whites are firm, pour in the hot syrup while continuing to beat at high speed. The volume of the beaten whites will expand considerably once the hot syrup is beaten in. Sprinkle on the cornstarch and beat again very briefly.

4. Spoon the soufflé batter into the prepared mold. Level off the top and with your thumb remove about ¼ inch of batter from around the edge of the dish; this will insure a straight-rising crown.

5. Place the dish in the hot oven, reduce the temperature to 375°, and bake for 15 to 20 minutes, or until the puffed top has darkened a little. Serve at once.

❀ Chocolate Omelet

total calories — 545 • per serving — 109

Even the novice who has difficulty with rolling omelets can easily prepare a puffy dessert omelet. The batter is completely baked in the oven, which eliminates any special techniques required for fast cooking and folding on the stove top.

Since Chocolate Omelets go so well with creams or sauces,

whipped evaporated skimmed milk is included in the calorie count. Other possibilities are Creamy Dessert Sauce (page 195) or Rum Sauce (page 199).

Serves 5

¼	cup evaporated skimmed milk	(48)
1	tablespoon butter	(102)
3	eggs, separated, room temperature	(231)
3	tablespoons sugar, sifted	(138)
2	teaspoons orange liqueur	(8)
1	teaspoon rum	(4)
	pinch of cream of tartar	——
1	tablespoon cocoa	(14)
½	teaspoon lemon juice	——

Preheat oven to 350°.

1. Pour the evaporated skimmed milk into a mixing bowl and place in the freezer for about 30 minutes, or until it begins to form ice crystals; also chill the beaters. Put the butter in a deep 9-inch pie dish (about 4-cup capacity) and place in the oven to melt the butter. Meanwhile, beat the yolks and 1½ tablespoons of sugar together until light and frothy. Add the orange liqueur and rum and beat again.

2. Add the cream of tartar to the egg whites and beat until the whites are frothy. Gradually add the remaining 1½ tablespoons of sugar to the whites and beat until they are firm and the peaks will stand up. Fold about one-third of the beaten whites into the yolks and blend well together. Add the remaining beaten whites to the yolk base and delicately fold in. Before the whites are completely incorporated, sprinkle on the cocoa and fold into the batter with the whites.

3. Use pot holders to remove the pie dish from the oven and rotate the dish so that the melted butter greases the entire surface. Scrape the omelet batter into the pie dish and place in the oven for about 10 minutes, or until the omelet is nice and puffy.

4. While the omelet is baking, whip the icy evaporated skimmed milk. Add the lemon juice to the milk and whip at high speed until it thickens and triples in volume. Flavor with a little sugar and orange liqueur or rum, if you like.

100

5. To serve: Bring the hot omelet to the table on a platter and pull it apart into individual portions with two large spoons. Serve on warm dishes and pass the whipped milk separately.

❀ Strawberry Omelet

total calories — 489 • per serving — 82

In the preceding recipe the Chocolate Omelet is baked. In this one it is fried. Both are puffy omelets, achieved by separating the eggs and folding in beaten whites. The ingredients are exactly the same as they would be for a regular rolled omelet, but by beating the whites the volume is expanded considerably. There are more servings per omelet, hence fewer calories. In this recipe the omelet is not fried until completely cooked, so the soft interior becomes a sauce as well.

Serves 6

FILLING:

½	cup strawberries (about 6)	(28)
¼	cup orange juice	(27)
1	teaspoon orange liqueur	(4)
1	teaspoon sugar	(15)
½	teaspoon cornstarch	(5)
2	teaspoons water	———

OMELET:

4	eggs, room temperature	(308)
1	tablespoon sugar	(46)
½	teaspoon orange liqueur	(2)
½	teaspoon vanilla	(3)
	pinch of cream of tartar	———
½	tablespoon butter	(51)

1. Cut the berries in half, or slice if very large. Place them in a small saucepot with the orange juice, orange liqueur, and sugar

and put aside to marinate for 15 minutes. Mix the cornstarch and water together in a small bowl or cup and stir into the berry sauce. Place the pot on medium heat and bring to the simmering point. Cook for about a minute until the sauce thickens a little and the starchy taste of the cornstarch disappears. Keep warm over very low heat or on a heat-deflector pad. The filling can be made ahead and refrigerated until needed, then reheated slowly.

2. Separate two of the eggs. Put the yolks and the remaining two whole eggs together in a bowl. Add ½ tablespoon of sugar, the orange liqueur, and vanilla and beat together lightly with a fork. Add the cream of tartar to the egg whites and beat until the whites are soft; add the remaining ½ tablespoon of sugar and beat until firm. Pour about one-half the beaten egg yolks over the whites and fold in well; then pour in the remaining yolks and fold in lightly.

3. Select a large nonstick frying pan, about 12 inches in diameter. Melt the butter and rotate the pan so the butter coats the entire surface. When the butter is hot, pour in the omelet batter and cook for about a minute. The bottom layer of the batter should be cooked and firm and lightly browned. Remove the pan from the heat and place the warm strawberry filling in the center; reserve 1 tablespoon of filling to garnish the top, if you like. Fold the omelet in half and slide onto a warm serving dish. Serve at once. (An alternate method of presenting the omelet is to spoon the filling over most of the surface of the omelet while it is cooking, then place a large, round serving platter over the top of the pan and invert. In this case the omelet will be round rather than folded. The soft sauce underneath is spooned up as the omelet is served.)

❀ Apple Omelet

total calories — 643 • per serving — 107

The omelet procedure is the same as for the preceding Strawberry Omelet; only the filling is different.

Serves 6

FILLING:

1	medium apple	(53)
½	tablespoon butter	(51)
1	tablespoon sugar	(46)
1	tablespoon apple juice	(7)
1	teaspoon brandy	(4)
2	tablespoons whipped cream cheese	(74)

OMELET:

4	eggs	(308)
1	tablespoon sugar	(46)
½	teaspoon vanilla	(3)
	pinch of cream of tartar	——
½	tablespoon butter	(51)

1. Peel the apple, cut into quarters, core, and slice thin. Melt the butter in a small pan, add the apples and sugar, and sauté for a few minutes until the slices become slightly transparent and are tender when pierced with a small, sharp knife. Add the apple juice, brandy, and whipped cream cheese. Reduce the heat to very low and stir until the cream cheese melts. Keep warm over very low heat or on a heat-deflector pad. The filling can be made ahead and refrigerated until needed, then reheated slowly.

2. Prepare the omelet according to directions in the preceding recipe for Strawberry Omelet and fill with the apple filling.

✿ Frozen Desserts

SMALL WONDER Americans are hooked on frozen desserts. Long before children can handle their first cone, they are spoon-fed ice cream. The addiction only intensifies over the years. As bad luck would have it, our appreciation of ice cream has grown while the commercially packaged product has deteriorated. Artificial sweeteners, artificial flavorings, and sturdy emulsifiers have largely replaced the wholesome ingredients some of us fondly remember. This drop in quality is largely responsible for the tremendous increase in homemade frozen sweets. Better ice-cream makers have helped this trend along. Electric machines are available at moderate prices — both the old-fashioned bucket model (some using regular ice cubes instead of crushed ice) and the iceless type that churns in the freezer of your refrigerator. These devices make better ice cream than can be made by freezing a mixture in ice-cube trays or mixing bowls. Still, even without an electrical appliance, excellent desserts are possible if the rules spelled out below are followed. A chemistry note: Not only do sugar and creams sweeten and enrich frozen desserts, but they also help prevent ice crystals from forming. The amount of both has been worked out in the following recipes to walk a narrow and slimming line.

❀ Café au Lait Glacé
(Frozen Coffee with Milk)

total calories — 470 • *per serving — 59*

If using instant coffee for this recipe, I urge you to use the espresso variety, because its strong flavor will better withstand dilution by other ingredients. The texture of this frozen dessert borders on that of the Italian *granite* (ices) and, like them, lends itself to a final fluffing with a fork or spoon just before serving.

Serves 8

2	cups strong coffee	
	or 2 cups water and 2 tablespoons instant coffee,	
	preferably freeze-dried espresso	(10)
6	tablespoons sugar	(276)
1	tablespoon rum	(12)
½	cup evaporated milk	(172)
	Optional: chocolate sprinkles for garnish	

1. Pour the coffee or water into a small pot, add the sugar, and bring to a boil. Reduce the heat to medium and simmer for 5 minutes.

2. Meanwhile, put the rum and, if using it, the instant coffee in a mixing bowl. Pour the hot syrup into the bowl and stir to dissolve the coffee. Put aside to cool for 5 minutes, then stir in the evaporated milk. Cool, then pour into an ice-cream freezer. Lacking an ice-cream freezer, pour the liquid into ice-cube trays and place in the freezer. As the mixture begins to freeze, stir from time to time, even reducing it almost to the liquid stage once or twice. The more frozen the dessert becomes, the more vigorously it should be beaten to keep it from freezing into a solid mass.

3. Beat the frozen coffee just before serving. Spoon into individual glasses — even tumblers will do. If desired, decorate each portion with a few chocolate sprinkles.

❀ Frozen Cups-of-Chocolate

total calories — 826 • per serving — 83

To most people a cup of anything really good is far more desirable than a whole pint of some bland, chemical-ladened concoction. Here is that cup, and scant though it is, no more is needed. The very first bite of its cool and darkly rich flavor satisfies completely.

Serves 10

1½	cups skimmed milk	(132)
2	teaspoons instant freeze-dried coffee	(2)
2	teaspoons rum	(8)
1	tablespoon sugar	(46)
4	ounces semisweet chocolate	(576)
¼	cup cocoa	(56)
1	teaspoon vanilla	(6)
10	2½-inch foil baking cups or other small cups	

1. Pour into a pot the milk, instant coffee, rum, and sugar. Place the pot on medium heat and bring to the boiling point.

2. Meanwhile, break or cut the chocolate into small chunks and place in the blender. Process to break up the chocolate into still smaller pieces. Add the cocoa.

3. When the milk comes to the boiling point, pour it into the blender, cover, and let stand for about 1 minute. Add the vanilla and process until the texture becomes smooth.

4. Have the cups ready on a baking sheet or tray that will fit into the freezer. Pour the chocolate liquid into the cups and freeze.

5. Remove from the freezer to the refrigerator about 15 minutes before serving.

❅ Frozen Creamed Pumpkin

total calories — 670 • *per serving — 112*

Quite naturally, one tends to think of pumpkin as a fall and winter fruit. But with the good-quality pumpkin available in cans, this rich-tasting squash can be enjoyed straight around the year. You'll find that, once frozen, the full flavor of the pumpkin and its complementary spices cools down most refreshingly.

Serves 6

1 cup apple juice	(117)
2 tablespoons maple syrup	(100)
2 tablespoons brown sugar	(68)
1 cup unsweetened pumpkin	(81)
½ teaspoon nutmeg	(6)
½ teaspoon cinnamon	(3)
½ teaspoon ginger	(3)
pinch of cloves	——
½ cup evaporated skimmed milk	(96)
½ cup evaporated milk	(172)
2 teaspoons brandy	(24)

1. In a pot, boil together for 5 minutes the apple juice, maple syrup, and brown sugar. Meanwhile, spoon the pumpkin into a mixing bowl and add the nutmeg, cinnamon, ginger, and cloves. Pour in the hot syrup and stir to blend it completely with the pumpkin. Set aside to cool for 15 minutes.

2. Stir in the evaporated skimmed milk, evaporated milk, and the brandy. Pour the pumpkin sauce into an ice-cream freezer or place the mixing bowl in the freezer. If the mixing bowl is used, the dessert must be beaten from time to time to prevent it from getting too icy.

3. Remove the bowl from the freezer to the refrigerator about 30 minutes before serving. Scoop into balls.

❀ Frozen Zabaglione

total calories — 522 • per serving — 131

Zabaglione (or *sabayon*) is best known as a liqueur-laced, warm dessert whipped together just before serving. But the same sauce, with whipped cream added, is often turned into a fine frozen confection. Several changes were necessary to trim the calories down to reasonable limits. Sugar was the obvious place to start, since most desserts are oversugared; then whipped evaporated milk replaced heavy cream; and finally, the liqueur was allowed to be heated through to dissipate most of its alcohol (read calories). Enough residual sugar remains from the alcohol to keep the Frozen Zabaglione velvety smooth.

Serves 4

½	cup evaporated milk	(172)
3	egg yolks	(186)
3	tablespoons sugar, sifted	(138)
2	tablespoons liqueur — amaretto, Marsala, Grand Marnier	(24)
2	teaspoons lemon juice	(2)

1. Pour the evaporated milk into a mixing bowl and place in the freezer to become slightly icy; also chill the beaters.

2. Place the yolks and sugar in a deep, heavy saucepan and beat together to blend. Put the saucepan on a heat-deflector pad over medium heat and continue beating until the mixture turns quite frothy and has doubled or tripled in volume. Beat constantly and, above all, do not hurry this step; success depends on the slow dissolving of the sugar into the yolks and the resulting expansion.

3. Gradually add the liqueur and beat for another minute. Scrape the sauce into a large mixing bowl and plunge the bottom of the bowl into cold water to stop any further cooking of the yolks. Continue beating until the mixture is cool.

4. Add the lemon juice to the icy milk and beat at high speed until the milk becomes very thick and triples in volume. (If you have only one set of beaters and have used them for the warm sauce, rinse them off well, first with warm water, then with cold,

and place in the freezer, still wet, for 2 or 3 minutes. The cool sauce can wait.) Scoop about one-third of the whipped milk into the sauce and beat in until thoroughly blended. Lightly fold in the rest of the whipped milk.

5. The classic preparation of zabaglione, warm or frozen, is in parfait or stemmed wine glasses. Pour the zabaglione into a pitcher, then carefully pour it into 4 individual serving glasses. Using the pitcher helps avoid having to wipe away messy dripping marks from the clear upper part of the glasses. Place in the freezer.

6. Remove the zabaglione from the freezer about 20 minutes before serving. Place each parfait glass on a saucer along with a spoon.

❧ Frozen Strawberry Zabaglione

total calories — 835 • *per serving — 139*

Because of the water content in strawberries, this fruit zabaglione will freeze too solid if left in the freezer a long time. About two hours is the limit.

Serves 6

¾	cup evaporated milk	(258)
1½	cups strawberries	(83)
4	egg yolks	(248)
⅓	cup sugar	(230)
1	tablespoon orange liqueur	(12)
1	tablespoon lemon juice	(4)

1. Pour the evaporated milk into a mixing bowl and place in the freezer to become slightly icy; also chill the beaters. Purée the strawberries in an electric blender or food processor; there should be about ¾ cup of purée.

2. Place the yolks and sugar in a deep, heavy saucepan and beat together to blend. Put the saucepan on a heat-deflector pad over medium heat and continue beating until the mixture turns quite

frothy and has doubled or tripled in volume. Beat constantly and, above all, do not hurry this step; success depends on the slow dissolving of the sugar into the yolks and the resulting expansion.

3. Gradually pour in the purée while continuing to beat. Add the orange liqueur and beat for another minute. Scrape the sauce into a large mixing bowl and plunge the bottom of the bowl into cold water to stop any further cooking of the yolks. Continue beating until the mixture is cool.

4. Add the lemon juice to the icy milk and beat at high speed until the milk becomes very thick and triples in volume. (If you have only one set of beaters, see note in Step 4 of the preceding recipe for Frozen Zabaglione.) Scoop about one-third of the whipped milk into the sauce and beat in until thoroughly blended. Lightly fold in the rest of the whipped milk.

5. The classic presentation of zabaglione, warm or frozen, is in parfait or stemmed wine glasses. Pour the zabaglione into a pitcher, then carefully pour it into 6 individual serving glasses. Using the pitcher helps avoid messy dripping marks that have to be wiped off the sides of the glasses. Place in the freezer for 1 hour, 2 at the most.

6. Remove from the freezer 15 minutes before serving. Place each parfait glass on a saucer together with a spoon.

❄ Frozen Banana Bonbons

total calories — 170 • per bonbon — 17–21

These bonbon-sized banana morsels make a most nutritious snack for the children as well as adding interest to the dessert table. They can decorate frozen creams or fruit arrangements, or can even be served all by themselves with after-dinner coffee, displacing the ubiquitous mint. Banana Bonbons do not freeze into an icy chunk, and they will keep for several months in the freezer.

Makes 8 to 10 bonbons

1 medium banana	(101)
3 tablespoons wheat germ	(69)
8 to 10 toothpicks	

110

1. Peel the banana, pull off any fibrous strings, and cut into ½-inch lengths. There will be 8 to 10 pieces, depending on the size of the banana.

2. Sprinkle some wheat germ into a saucer and roll each piece of banana in it, patting to make the coating stick. Keep adding wheat germ to the saucer as needed.

3. Stick a toothpick through the side of each piece (which is firmer than the center) and place on a dish. Freeze for at least 3 hours.

4. To serve: Remove from the freezer 5 minutes before eating.

❀ Ginger Granita

total calories — 404 • per serving — 67

Fruit *granite* are certainly refreshing, but they cannot begin to compare to the crisp, tingling flavor of fresh ginger ice. In fact, this cooling delight could do service as a palate refresher between courses of a large formal dinner — a *trou normand,* as the French would say. That term has come to mean various sherbets served mid-meal, but originally meant a shot of Calvados, which at times can indeed burn a hole (*trou*).

Thanks to the current vogue for Chinese cooking, fresh ginger can be found in most large supermarkets as well as oriental specialty shops. Don't be tempted to substitute powdered ginger. I've worked out the recipe both ways — this one works, the other doesn't.

Serves 6

½ ounce fresh ginger root (about 1½ inches)	(7)
½ cup sugar	(385)
2 cups water	——
1-inch piece orange rind	——
1 tablespoon vodka	(12)
Optional: candied ginger or Candied Orange Peel (page 43) for garnish	

1. Cut the unpeeled ginger root into thin slices and put in a small pot with the sugar, water, and orange rind. Place the pot over medium-high heat and once the liquid comes to a boil, allow it to simmer briskly for 5 minutes, uncovered. Remove the pot from the fire, add the vodka, cover, and put aside to steep for 15 minutes.

2. Place a strainer over a mixing bowl and pour the ginger syrup into it; discard the ginger and orange rind. Cool the syrup, then pour it into an ice-cream freezer or ice-cube trays placed in the freezing compartment.

3. If the freezing is being done in trays, beat the granita from time to time. It will not freeze into a solid mass.

4. Fluff up the granita with a wooden spoon just before serving and scoop into individual bowls. If desired, garnish with a thin slice of candied ginger or a few strands of Candied Orange Peel.

Champagne Ice

total calories — 1319 • per serving — 165

Alcohol is liberally sprinkled throughout this book because in most recipes it is cooked, which drives off the alcohol with all its calories. Even though a whole bottle of champagne is used in this festive dessert and is not cooked, the final calorie count is still less than you would expect. This is the happy result of churning the champagne into an ice, adding no cream, egg yolks, or rich flavorings. It is the flavor of the champagne that dominates, as it should.

Serves 8

¾	*cup sugar*	*(577)*
¾	*cup water*	——
	pinch of salt	——
½	*cup orange juice*	*(54)*
	juice of 1 lemon	*(20)*
1	*bottle champagne, chilled*	*(653)*
1	*egg white, lightly beaten*	*(15)*
	Optional: for each glass, 1 crystallized violet or a few strands of Candied Orange Peel (page 43) for garnish	

1. Boil the sugar, water, and salt together for about 5 minutes, uncovered. Add the orange and lemon juice and bring back to a boil; immediately remove the pot from the heat and cool.

2. Pour the cool syrup into a large mixing bowl and stir in ½ the bottle of champagne. Place the bowl in the freezer. As the mixture begins to freeze, beat it with a wire whisk or wooden spoon to break up the ice crystals and to give a fluffy look to the finished ice. Do this several times.

3. Add the egg white and remaining half-bottle of champagne. Return the bowl to the freezer. Beat from time to time, trying to maintain its fluffiness. Champagne Ice will never freeze into a solid mass, but will remain much like snow; the alcohol works as antifreeze.

4. Chill individual champagne or other stemmed wine glasses. At the last moment, spoon the Champagne Ice into the glasses.

❀ Rosé Snow

total calories — 396 • *per serving — 66*

The food processor makes superfast work of producing ices and snows. No beating is necessary during the freezing, and the final result is still light and fluffy. The rosé wine used in this recipe emerges from the processor a pale pink delicacy.

Serves 6

⅓ cup sugar	(230)
⅓ cup water	——
pinch of salt	——
2 cups slightly sweet rosé wine	(100)
½ cup unsweetened peach nectar	(60)
⅛ teaspoon nutmeg	(2)
1 tablespoon lemon juice	(4)

1. In a 1-quart saucepot, boil together the sugar, water, and salt for 5 minutes. Remove the pot from the heat and stir in the rosé wine, peach nectar, nutmeg, and lemon juice. Return the pot to the heat and bring back to a boil. Immediately remove the pot from the heat and cool.

2. Pour the rosé syrup into an ice-cube tray equipped with the cube dividers. Freeze.

3. Just before serving, place the metal blade in the food processor container, add the cubes, and process, turning on and off rapidly. The frozen rosé cubes will turn into a fine-grained ice. Serve immediately in chilled dessert bowls.

❀ Frozen Fruit Creams

No doubt about it, marshmallows are sweet. But then, no other sugar is added to these desserts. Because of their fluffy bulk they also happen to be great stretchers of recipes; a given quantity serves several extra people. Marshmallows will also beautifully emulsify a frozen dessert, keeping it creamy smooth. Here are basic recipes for bananas and peaches, the latter in both summer and winter versions. Substitute other fruits of the season.

❀ Frozen Banana Cream

total calories — 1307 • per serving — 131
with garnish — 140

Serves 10

¼	cup water	——
1	tablespoon kirsch	(12)
8	oz. (about 24 large) marshmallows	(552)
2	cups banana purée (5 or 6 bananas)	(382)
4	tablespoons lemon juice	(16)
1	cup evaporated milk	(345)
	Optional: 1 small banana and ¼ cup orange juice for garnish	

1. Put a nonaluminum pot on a heat-deflector pad and pour in the water and kirsch. Add the marshmallows, turn the heat to medium, and melt them slowly, stirring occasionally.

2. Meanwhile, purée the bananas in a blender or food processor

and pour them into a large mixing bowl. Add 2 tablespoons lemon juice and stir. Pour in the melted marshmallows and beat for a half-minute with a wire whisk. Chill well.

3. During this time, pour the evaporated milk into a mixing bowl and put it in the freezer until ice crystals begin to form; also chill the beaters. Add the remaining 2 tablespoons of lemon juice to the milk and beat at high speed until it triples in volume and is quite firm. Fold about one-third of the whipped milk into the banana purée and blend thoroughly. Add the remaining whipped milk and delicately fold it into the mixture.

4. Lightly oil an 8-cup mold (a loaf pan works very well) and spoon in the banana cream. Tap the mold on the table a few times to settle the cream well into the container. Freeze.

5. If the garnish is used, about 15 minutes before serving cut the banana diagonally to produce elongated slices; put them in a small bowl, pour in the orange juice, and turn the slices until they are all coated with the juice. This will prevent them from turning dark. At serving time, line a chilled platter with a neatly folded white dish towel and unmold the frozen cream onto it. (The towel will prevent the dessert from sliding while being cut.)

6. Lift the banana slices out of the orange juice and, if a rectangular mold is used, arrange them in an overlapping row down the center; or decorate according to the shape of the mold.

❄ Frozen Peach Cream I

total calories — 1150 • per serving — 115
with garnish — 119

Serves 10

¼ cup water	——
8 ounces (about 24 large) marshmallows	(552)
1 tablespoon orange liqueur	(12)
1½ pounds ripe peaches (about 5 or 6)	(225)
4 tablespoons lemon juice	(16)
1 cup evaporated milk	(345)
Optional: 1 peach, peeled and sliced, for garnish	

1. Put a nonaluminum pot on a heat-deflector pad and pour in the water. Add the marshmallows, turn the heat to medium, and melt them slowly, stirring occasionally. When the marshmallows have melted, stir in the orange liqueur.

2. Meanwhile, peel the peaches, cut into chunks, and purée them in an electric blender or food processor. Pour the purée into a large mixing bowl, add 2 tablespoons of lemon juice, and stir. Pour in the melted marshmallows and beat for a half-minute with a wire whisk. Chill well.

3. While the purée is cooling, pour the evaporated milk into a mixing bowl and put it in the freezer until ice crystals begin to form; also chill the beaters. Add the remaining 2 tablespoons of lemon juice to the icy milk and beat at high speed until it triples in volume and is quite firm. Fold about one-third of the whipped milk into the peach purée and blend thoroughly. Add the remaining whipped milk and delicately fold it into the mixture.

4. Lightly oil an 8-cup mold (a loaf pan, ring mold, or soufflé dish work well) and spoon in the peach mixture. Tap the mold on the table a few times to settle the cream well into the container. Freeze.

5. To serve: Line a chilled platter with a neatly folded white dish towel and unmold the frozen cream onto it. (The towel will prevent the dessert from sliding while being cut.) Decorate with the optional sliced peach, if desired.

✿ Frozen Peach Cream II

total calories — 539 • per serving — 90

This version of Frozen Peach Cream is intended for those months when the lush flavor of the fresh fruit is a sweet memory.

Serves 6

2	*tablespoons water*	——
3	*ounces (about 9 large) marshmallows*	(207)
1	*tablespoon orange liqueur*	(12)
16	*ounces unsweetened canned peaches, drained*	(140)
2	*tablespoons lemon juice*	(8)
½	*cup evaporated milk*	(172)

1. Put a nonaluminum pot on a heat-deflector pad and pour in the water. Add the marshmallows, turn the heat to medium, and melt them slowly, stirring occasionally. When they have melted, stir in the orange liqueur.

2. Meanwhile, reserve 3 or 4 peach slices and purée the rest of the peaches in the blender with 1 tablespoon of lemon juice. Pour the purée into a mixing bowl, add the melted marshmallows, and beat for a half-minute with a wire whisk. Chill well.

3. While the purée is cooling, pour the evaporated milk into a mixing bowl and put it in the freezer until ice crystals begin to form; also chill the beaters. Add the remaining tablespoon of lemon juice to the icy milk and beat at high speed until it triples in volume and is quite firm. Fold about one-third of the whipped milk into the peach purée and blend thoroughly. Add the remaining whipped milk and delicately fold it into the mixture.

4. Lightly oil a 6-cup mold (loaf pan, ring mold, or soufflé dish) and spoon in the peach mixture. Tap the mold on the table a few times to settle the cream well into the container. Freeze.

5. To serve: Line a chilled platter with a neatly folded white dish towel and unmold the frozen cream onto it. Decorate with the reserved peach slices.

✤ Citrus Sherbets

Citrus sherbets can be used in a variety of ways — as simply a dish of sherbet, as a base for sliced fresh fruit, or, most elegantly of all, as the heart of a Champagne Fruit Cup (page 42). These sherbets will be quite pale in color, almost white, in fact; this is just as they should be. Please don't be tempted to add any coloring.

✿ Lemon Sherbet

total calories — 825 • per serving — 103

Serves 8

3	or 4 lemons (enough for ½ cup lemon juice)	(32)
1	cup sugar	(770)
3½	cups water	——
1	tablespoon gelatin	(23)
	pinch of salt	——

1. With a swivel-bladed vegetable peeler, remove the rind from the lemons; be careful to remove the rind only and none of the white pith beneath. Cut into very thin juliennes while bringing 4 cups of water to a boil. Add the sliced rind and boil rapidly for about 3 minutes. Drain and cool in cold water at once. Drain again, place in a small bowl, cover, and refrigerate.

2. Boil the sugar and 3¼ cups water together in a small pot for 5 minutes. Meanwhile, soften the gelatin in ¼ cup of water. Squeeze the lemons and strain the juice.

3. Stir the softened gelatin into the hot syrup to dissolve. Add a pinch of salt and the lemon juice. Cool, then place in an ice-cream maker or, lacking one, an ice-cube tray placed in the freezer. Stir from time to time during the freezing process, and at least once (twice is better) beat the mixture with a wire whisk until it is mushy.

4. Remove from freezer at least 20 minutes before serving. Using either an ice-cream scoop or sturdy tablespoon to scrape the frosty sherbet, fill individual bowls and then decorate with the blanched rind.

✿ Lime Sherbet

total calories — 825 • per serving — 103

Serves 8

10	to 12 limes (enough for ½ cup juice)	(32)
1	cup sugar	(770)
3½	cups water	——

1 tablespoon gelatin	(23)
pinch of salt	——

Follow the directions in the preceding recipe for Lemon Sherbet, except that you may want to mix some lemon rind with the lime rind for the garnish. The green of the lime dulls during the blanching, whereas the lemon remains quite fresh in color.

❀ Orange Milk Sherbet

total calories — 763 • per serving — 95

Serves 8

1 cup skimmed milk	(88)
½ tablespoon gelatin	(12)
1 cup evaporated skimmed milk	(192)
2 tablespoons sugar	(92)
¾ cup frozen orange juice (1 6-ounce can)	(363)
1 teaspoon grated orange rind (optional)	——
1 teaspoon lemon juice	(1)
1 egg white, room temperature	(15)

1. Pour ½ cup skimmed milk into a small bowl, sprinkle on the gelatin, and set aside to soften. Put the remaining ½ cup of skimmed milk and the cup of evaporated skimmed milk into a pot, place on medium heat, and bring just to the boiling point. Remove the pot from the heat and immediately add the softened gelatin and stir until completely dissolved. Add the sugar. Cool the milk mixture until slightly syrupy.

2. Pour the undiluted frozen orange juice into a large mixing bowl; add the lemon juice, milk syrup, and, if desired, the optional grated orange rind. With an electric beater, whip the mixture until it is smooth and fluffy. Place in the freezer until mushy.

3. Lightly beat the egg white. Whip the orange milk again with the beater, add the egg white, and beat again. Return to the freezer and freeze until firm. Whipping once more will improve the texture but is not essential. Remove the bowl from the freezer about 15 minutes before serving.

❅ Grapefruit Sherbet

total calories — 467 • per serving — 78

The typical American view of grapefruit is through sleepy eyes at the breakfast table. Too bad, since the sharp-tasting citrus can deliver a lot of flavor punch at other meals as well. This tangy sherbet is only one example. Though it makes a most refreshing end to a meal, grapefruit sherbet could also be used as a palate refreshener midway through a large formal meal.

Serves 6

2	cups fresh grapefruit sections or 1 16-ounce can unsweetened grapefruit sections	*(146)*
½	cup unsweetened grapefruit juice (1¼ cups if using fresh grapefruit)	*(51)*
	juice of ½ lemon	*(10)*
	pinch of salt	——
⅓	cup sugar	*(230)*
2	egg whites, room temperature	*(30)*
	pinch of cream of tartar	——
	Optional: grapefruit rind for garnish*	

1. If using canned grapefruit, drain the sections and reserve the juice; there should be about ¾ cup. In a saucepot, combine the drained juice with the additional ½ cup of grapefruit juice. If fresh grapefruit is used, start with 1¼ cups of fresh grapefruit juice in the saucepot. Add the lemon juice, salt, and sugar, bring to a boil, reduce the heat, and simmer briskly for 5 minutes.

2. While the syrup is boiling, place the grapefruit sections in the container of an electric blender or food processor and process until very smooth. Add the cream of tartar to the egg whites in a large mixing bowl and beat the whites with an electric beater until firm but not stiff.

---

* Optional garnish: Grapefruit rind can be candied according to the directions for Candied Orange Peel (page 43) and kept tightly covered in the refrigerator. Scatter a few pieces over the top of each serving, or over the sherbet on the platter.

3. Slowly pour the hot syrup over the whites while continuing to beat at medium speed. Switch to high speed and beat until the whites are smooth, stiff, and glossy. Slowly add the puréed grapefruit, pouring it against the side of the bowl, while beating at medium speed.

4. Pour the mixture into an ice-cream churner and freeze, or place the bowl in the freezer. In the latter case, beat the sherbet with the electric beater three or four times during the freezing process, waiting for it to freeze to the mushy stage between beatings. At first it will separate, but will smooth out by the third beating, after which it can either remain in the bowl or be transferred to a 5-cup mold. Place the container in the freezer for several hours, or until the sherbet is frozen. Remove it from the freezer about 15 minutes before serving. If a mold is used, turn the sherbet onto a chilled platter.

❀ Frozen Yogurts

It might very well be asked why one should bother making frozen yogurts when they can be bought so easily. The answer lies in the calorie count. Though food producers may begin with a low-fat yogurt, by the time they have "improved" it with lots of sugar, syrups, jams, and jellies, and all sorts of stabilizers, that pure beginning suddenly becomes absolutely sinful. Eight ounces of homemade Frozen Strawberry Yogurt, for example, carry only 133 calories, but when the same amount is spooned out of the package, you can figure on anywhere from 210 to 270. Below are several recipes to begin with, using basically the same technique. These frozen yogurts are best served by either scraping with a heavy tablespoon or a scoop containing sealed antifreeze. Experiment with your favorite fruits and flavors and save both money and calories.

❄ Frozen Strawberry Yogurt

total calories — 546 • per serving — 91

Serves 6

¼	cup orange juice	*(27)*
¼	cup sugar	*(192)*
¼	cup water	——
1	tablespoon gelatin	*(23)*
2	cups strawberries	*(110)*
1½	cups plain low-fat yogurt	*(194)*

1. Boil the orange juice and sugar together in a small pot for 5 minutes. Meanwhile, pour the water into a small cup, sprinkle on the gelatin, and put aside to soften. When the juice has finished boiling, remove the pot from the heat and stir in the gelatin until dissolved. Cool slightly.

2. Put the strawberries and yogurt in the container of a blender or food processor and purée the berries. With the motor running, slowly pour in the orange juice syrup, then continue processing for another few seconds; there should be about 4 cups. Pour the fruit yogurt into an ice-cream freezer, or into ice-cube trays that are then placed in the freezer. As ice crystals begin to form, fluff the yogurt with a fork. Repeat this process three or four times.

3. To serve: Remove the frozen yogurt from the freezer 20 to 25 minutes before serving and beat again with a fork to fluff up the mixture. Spoon into individual serving bowls.

❄ Frozen Apple Yogurt

total calories — 678 • per serving — 113

Serves 6

½	cup unsweetened apple juice	*(59)*
¼	cup sugar	*(192)*
1	tablespoon gelatin	*(23)*
2	cups unsweetened applesauce	*(200)*
1½	cups plain low-fat yogurt	*(194)*

¼	teaspoon cinnamon	(2)
¼	teaspoon nutmeg	(3)
½	teaspoon vanilla	(3)
½	tablespoon lemon juice	(2)

Follow directions in preceding recipe for Frozen Strawberry Yogurt, but soften the gelatin in ¼ cup of the apple juice instead of water. The dessert can be made without a blender. Beat together in a bowl the apple sauce, yogurt, and flavorings. Add the hot syrup and beat again vigorously.

❀ Frozen Banana Yogurt

total calories — 566 • per serving — 94

Serves 6

¼	cup unsweetened pineapple juice or banana nectar	(35)
¼	cup sugar	(192)
¼	cup water	——
1	tablespoon gelatin	(23)
1	large banana	(116)
1½	cups plain low-fat yogurt	(194)
1	teaspoon vanilla	(6)

Follow directions in Frozen Strawberry Yogurt recipe (page 122), adding vanilla after the hot syrup has been incorporated.

❀ Frozen Blueberry Yogurt

total calories — 620 • per serving — 103

Serves 6

¼	cup orange juice	(27)
¼	cup sugar	(192)
¼	cup water	——
1	tablespoon gelatin	(23)
2	cups blueberries	(180)
1	tablespoon lemon juice	(4)
1½	cups plain low-fat yogurt	(194)

Follow directions in Frozen Strawberry Yogurt recipe (page 122). Unsweetened frozen blueberries may be substituted for fresh berries, but they must be thawed and rinsed before being measured.

❈ Frozen Blackberry Yogurt

total calories — 604 • *per serving — 101*

Serves 6

¼ cup orange juice	*(27)*
¼ cup sugar	*(192)*
¼ cup water	——
1 tablespoon gelatin	*(23)*
2 cups blackberries (thawed, if frozen)	*(168)*
1½ cups plain low-fat yogurt	*(194)*

Follow directions in Frozen Strawberry Yogurt recipe (page 122). Straining is necessary to remove the many small seeds. It is best to do this after all ingredients are blended together and the mixture is quite thin; strain directly into the freezing bowl.

❈ Frozen Honey Yogurt

total calories — 369 • *per serving — 92*

Serves 4

½ cup evaporated skimmed milk	*(96)*
2 tablespoons honey	*(128)*
½ tablespoon gelatin	*(12)*
1 cup plain low-fat yogurt	*(130)*
½ teaspoon vanilla	*(3)*
pinch of nutmeg	——

Follow directions in Frozen Strawberry Yogurt recipe (page 122), using ¼ cup evaporated skimmed milk to heat with the honey and the remaining ¼ cup to soften the gelatin. Blend the yogurt with the vanilla and nutmeg before pouring in the warm milk with honey and gelatin.

❀ Frozen Coffee Yogurt

total calories — 384 • per serving — 96

Serves 4

1 cup water	——
3 tablespoons sugar	(138)
1 tablespoon instant coffee, preferably freeze-dried	(5)
¼ cup skimmed milk	(22)
1 tablespoon gelatin	(23)
1 cup plain low-fat yogurt	(130)
1 teaspoon vanilla	(6)
1 tablespoon corn syrup	(60)

Follow directions in Frozen Strawberry Yogurt recipe (page 122), but soften the gelatin in the skimmed milk. The dessert can be made without a blender. Boil together the water, sugar, and coffee, then add the softened gelatin. Spoon the yogurt into a mixing bowl and pour the hot syrup over it while beating vigorously. Add the vanilla and corn syrup and beat again.

❦ Cookies

COOKIES PLAY a variety of roles in the daily diet. Following a heavy meal, a single Fudge or Butterscotch Brownie will often suffice for dessert. A thin, plain cookie, such as a Vanilla Crisp, is always tucked beside a dish of frozen creams or sherbets in any true French restaurant. In Belgium it would be unthinkable to serve hot drinks without a wafer similar to Belgian Spice Crisps. With cold milk at bedtime or for an afternoon snack, cookies such as Sesame Seed Lace make an ideal companion, an especially nutritious and energy-packed sweet.

The calories in store-bought cookies range as low as the mid-30s and zoom to to 250. Not a single cookie presented here touches even 50 calories, and one dips down to 18. But even the lowest of the low-calorie packaged cookies brings you much else: artificial flavorings and sweeteners, saturated fats and oils, preservatives, at times even coloring agents, and always an excess of sugars. How much better it is to control exactly what goes into the cookie batter yourself, especially when they are so easy to make, some even in the food processor. There is also a wonderful calorie-free bonus — a house full of fragrant aromas.

❧ Belgian Spice Crisps

total calories — 1871 • per cookie — 23

From the fanciest tearoom to the simplest café, it is a tradition in Belgium to serve paper-thin cookies with hot chocolate, coffee, or tea. Always fragrant with a medley of spices, these dark wafers add immeasurably to the enjoyment of any steaming cup. Though machines are employed in Belgian bakeries to achieve the necessary thinness, a good rolling pin plus a sheet of aluminum foil and a sheet of wax paper can produce the same results at home. The crackling, crisp quality of the cookies gives such a satisfying crunch when bitten into that it seemed a shame not to savor it in other aromas. I have switched the flavorings from spice to vanilla, ginger, and cocoa — among others — to produce a whole range of tastes. The color of the dough changes too, from a pale, pale lemony hue to nutty brown. Whatever the scent, though, all these cookies dislike humidity; keep them in airtight containers. Storage won't be much of a problem, since they disappear fast.

Makes about 80 2-inch cookies

6	tablespoons butter	(612)
2	tablespoons sugar	(92)
¼	cup dark corn syrup	(240)
1	teaspoon grated lemon rind	——
1	tablespoon lemon juice	(4)
1	teaspoon rum	(4)
¼	teaspoon each ginger, nutmeg, cloves, cinnamon	(9)
2	cups flour	(910)

1. Cream the butter and sugar together until light and fluffy. Add the corn syrup, lemon rind and juice, rum, and spices and beat well. Gradually stir in the flour until the dough forms a ball. (The dough can be prepared in a food processor, using the same procedure.) If the flour has been packed closely in the measuring cup, you may find that the dough tends not to cohere into a ball. The addition of a teaspoon or two of water will correct the proportions.

2. Divide the dough in two and pat each piece into a rec-

tangular shape. Wrap and chill for 1 or 2 hours in the refrigerator or place in the freezer for 15 minutes.

Preheat oven to 350°.

3. Measure out a large piece of aluminum foil that will fit a cookie sheet. Turn its shiny side down, place one of the rectangles of dough on it, and rap it a few times with a rolling pin to soften the chilled dough a little. Cover with a piece of wax paper the same length as the foil and fasten the two sheets together with several straight pins. Roll the dough between the foil and the wax paper as thin as you can. The thinner the better and crisper. Do not attempt to work too fast, but press down heavily on the rolling pin. The rolled-out dough should almost reach the edges of the wax paper.

4. Lift the dough with the foil and wax paper onto the cookie sheet, foil side down. Remove the straight pins and carefully pull off the wax paper. Cut the dough into any shape you desire — squares, rectangles, diamonds, triangles — but leave in place after cutting. Make certain you cut through the dough; this will prevent excess breakage later. Place in the oven for about 10 minutes, or until the cookies are lightly browned. The ultrathin dough at the edges of the pan will brown faster than the rest.

5. Repeat with the other half of the dough. Store in an airtight container. These crisps are not only extremely good, but very fragile as well. Avoid excessive handling. (Note: The second portion of dough can be frozen for future use.)

❊ Vanilla Crisps

total calories — 1771 • per cookie — 22

These delicately flavored cookies are perfect to serve with frozen desserts, puddings, and fruit. Because the vanilla essence seems to ripen if left to stand awhile, they are best made the day before.

Makes about 80 2-inch cookies

6	tablespoons butter	(612)
2	tablespoons sugar	(92)

2 tablespoons corn syrup	(120)
2 tablespoons vanilla	(36)
⅛ teaspoon nutmeg	(1)
2 cups flour	(910)

Follow directions in preceding recipe for Belgian Spice Crisps, adding the vanilla and nutmeg before stirring in the flour.

❀ Lemon Crisps

total calories — 1742 • per cookie — 22

Makes about 80 2-inch cookies

6 tablespoons butter	(612)
2 tablespoons sugar	(92)
2 tablespoons corn syrup	(120)
rind of 1 lemon, grated	——
2 tablespoons lemon juice	(8)
2 cups flour	(910)

Follow directions in Belgian Spice Crisps recipe (page 127), adding the lemon rind and juice before stirring in the flour.

❀ Cocoa Crisps

total calories — 1897 • per cookie — 24

Makes about 80 2-inch cookies

6 tablespoons butter	(612)
2 tablespoons sugar	(92)
2 tablespoons cocoa	(28)
¼ cup dark corn syrup	(240)
1½ teaspoons vanilla	(9)
1 teaspoon rum	(4)
¼ teaspoon cinnamon	(2)
2 cups flour	(910)

Follow directions in Belgian Spice Crisps recipe (page 127), adding all flavorings before stirring in the flour.

✺ Carob Crisps

total calories — 1950 • per cookie — 24

Makes about 80 2-inch cookies

6	tablespoons butter	(612)
2	tablespoons sugar	(92)
¼	cup dark corn syrup	(240)
3	tablespoons carob powder	(81)
2	teaspoons vanilla	(12)
¼	teaspoon nutmeg	(3)
2	cups flour	(910)

Follow directions in Belgian Spice Crisps recipe (page 127), adding all flavorings before stirring in the flour.

✺ Honey Crisps

total calories — 1886 • per cookie — 24

Makes about 80 2-inch cookies

6	tablespoons butter	(612)
2	tablespoons sugar	(92)
¼	cup honey	(256)
¼	teaspoon cinnamon	(2)
1	teaspoon amaretto liqueur or almond extract	(2)
2	teaspoons vanilla	(12)
2	cups flour	(910)

Follow directions in Belgian Spice Crisps recipe (page 127), adding all flavorings before stirring in the flour.

✣ Ginger Crisps

total calories — 1927 • per cookie   24

Makes about 80 2-inch cookies

6	tablespoons butter	(612)
2	tablespoons sugar	(92)
¼	cup dark corn syrup	(240)
1	teaspoon grated lemon rind	——
1	tablespoon lemon juice	(4)
1	teaspoon rum	(4)
1½	teaspoons powdered ginger	(9)
2	cups plus 2 tablespoons flour	(966)

Follow directions in Belgian Spice Crisps recipe (page 127), adding all flavorings before stirring in the flour.

✣ Maple Crisps

total calories — 1834 • per cookie — 23

Makes about 80 2-inch cookies

6	tablespoons butter	(612)
2	tablespoons sugar	(92)
¼	cup pure maple syrup	(200)
2	teaspoons rum	(8)
2	teaspoons vanilla	(12)
2	cups flour	(910)

Follow directions in Belgian Spice Crisps recipe (page 127), adding all flavorings before stirring in the flour.

❋ Sesame Seed Lace

total calories — 432 • per cookie — 18

Because of all the protein in sesame seeds, these thin cookies
are not only filling, but nutritious. The seeds are barely bound
together with egg and honey, so their toasted nutty flavor dominates. More cinnamon can be added if you would like to emphasize a Middle Eastern flavor.

Makes about 24 1½-inch cookies

1	egg	(77)
1	tablespoon honey	(64)
1	teaspoon vanilla	(6)
½	teaspoon cinnamon	(3)
1	teaspoon grated orange rind	——
6	tablespoons sesame seeds	(282)

Preheat oven to 350°.

1. Beat the egg with a fork in a mixing bowl. Add the honey
and beat well to blend the two together. Add the vanilla, cinnamon, and orange rind and beat well again. Stir in the sesame
seeds.

2. Place a sheet of parchment paper on a cookie sheet. A nonstick cookie sheet can be used if parchment paper is not available,
but wax paper cannot be used. Drop scant teaspoons of the mixture on the paper about 2 inches apart. Use the back of a teaspoon to spread the mixture until the seeds are in a single layer;
a rotating motion is the most efficient. Bake for 8 to 10 minutes,
or until the outer edge is a dark tan color and the centers of the
cookies feel crisp. If a nonstick sheet has been used, the cookies
must be removed while still hot. Once cool, keep in an airtight
container.

❀ Sesame Seed Cookies

total calories — 1200 • per cookie — 33

This is a very pretty and tasty cookie. The sesame seed coating bakes to a honey color, just a bit darker than the cookie dough beneath. The seeds also add a bit of a nutty flavor. I prefer to buy them in health food shops, where they are generally fresher and cheaper than those in small supermarket jars.

During the rolling and dipping of the cookies, a quick hand is needed. If the dough is allowed to sit in the water too long it will get soggy. I find that working with three cookies at a time is most efficient. It is also advisable not to pour all the sesame seeds into the dish at once, because they get wet when the cookies are rolled in them and they tend to clump together. It is much better to keep adding them from time to time, assuring a constant supply of dry seeds.

Makes about 3 dozen 1-inch cookies

4	tablespoons butter	(408)
2	tablespoons sugar	(92)
1	egg white	(15)
1	teaspoon vanilla	(6)
¼	teaspoon nutmeg	(3)
1	cup flour	(455)
	pinch of salt	――
½	teaspoon baking powder	(3)
¼	cup sesame seeds	(218)
¾	cup ice water	――

1. Cream the butter and sugar together very well until the mixture is light and fluffy. Add the egg white, vanilla, and nutmeg and mix well. Sift the flour, salt, and baking powder together and gradually work the dry ingredients into the butter and sugar. When the flour has been worked in, knead for a few minutes until the dough forms a smooth ball. If the dough seems too stiff, add a few drops of water. Chill for at least ½ hour.

   Preheat oven to 325°.

2. Put the ice water in a small bowl, and some of the sesame

seeds in a shallow saucer. Have two forks ready. With a teaspoon, take a small piece of the dough and roll it into a small, smooth ball between your palms. Hold this ball on a fork and dip it into the water for a few seconds; lift out and hold for a second to let excess water drip off. Immediately drop the cookie into the saucer of sesame seeds. With the second fork, roll the dough ball around in the seeds. Then transfer the ball to a nonstick or lightly greased cookie sheet, lightly pressing in the seeds as you do. (By keeping one fork for the water only, and the other for the seeds, you don't end up with a messy mixture of the two.)

3. Bake for 25 to 30 minutes, or until the seeds have turned a nice golden color.

✿ Almond Cookies

total calories — 1511 • per cookie — 42

The Chinese make these cookies by using half butter and half lard, which is higher calorically than butter. When only butter is used, as here, many calories are saved. An almond pressed into the top of each cookie is traditional, but nuts are rich and used in a limited way in this book. That last little touch, as much as 4 or 5 calories, is up to you.

Makes about 3 dozen 1¼-inch cookies

⅓ cup (5 tablespoons) butter	(510)
½ cup sugar	(385)
1 egg	(77)
2 teaspoons almond extract	(16)
1½ cups sifted cake flour	(523)
½ teaspoon baking soda	——
Optional: 18 blanched almonds for garnish	

1. Cream together the butter and sugar. Add the egg and almond extract and continue beating until all the ingredients are thoroughly blended.

2. Sift the cake flour, measure, and resift with baking soda.

Add the flour gradually to the batter, stirring with a wooden spoon to incorporate all the flour before adding more. Cover and chill the dough for at least 1 hour in the refrigerator or 20 minutes in the freezer.

Preheat oven to 350°.

3. Have a nonstick cookie sheet ready, or lightly grease a regular cookie sheet. Break off about a heaping teaspoon of the batter and roll between your palms into a ball about the size of a small walnut. Place on the sheet about 1½ inches apart.

4. Select a small glass with a flat bottom about the size of a fifty-cent piece. Wet the end of a dish towel and wrap it around the bottom of the glass, pulling the towel taut. Pressing the glass down on each cookie, spread all of them to an equal size; do not spread too thin. If optional almond garnish is used, split the almond in half lengthwise and press an almond half into the center of each cookie. Bake in the preheated oven for 12 to 13 minutes, or until the cookies are a nice golden brown.

❀ Poppyseed Cookies

total calories — 1416 • per cookie — 30

Poppyseed is generally used as a filling, a rich one. The tasty seeds are used with a sparing hand in this recipe. There are just enough to make dark speckles in the pale batter and add a crunchy texture to the cookie. The cookies are extremely easy to make and they freeze well.

Makes about 4 dozen 1½-inch cookies

1 egg	(77)
½ cup sugar	(385)
4 tablespoons butter, melted and cooled	(408)
¼ cup orange juice	(27)
1 teaspoon vanilla	(6)
⅛ teaspoon salt	——
2 tablespoons poppyseeds	(94)
1 cup sifted flour	(419)

135

Preheat oven to 350°.

1. Beat the egg until light and foamy, then add the sugar, melted butter, orange juice, vanilla, and salt. Beat again until the mixture is smooth and well blended.

2. Stir in the poppyseeds and finally the flour. Beat for a half-minute.

3. Use a nonstick or lightly greased regular cookie sheet. With a teaspoon, scoop up about a heaping ½ teaspoon of batter and with a second spoon, scrape the batter onto the cookie sheet. Space the cookies 1 inch apart. Place in the preheated oven and bake for about 15 minutes, or until the edges are a dark golden brown. The cookies will have spread to a flat shape. Remove immediately from the sheet.

❀ Viennese Crescents

total calories — 1895 • per crescent — 32

The secret here is freshly chopped almonds. If you try using packaged almond powder or bits, you will end up with no flavor at all. The blender or the food processor, especially, makes quick work of the chore. The next best device is the spring-loaded hand chopper, operated by pushing the handle that drives the blades down.

Makes about 60 1½-inch crescents

4	*tablespoons butter*	*(408)*
3	*tablespoons sugar*	*(138)*
2	*teaspoons vanilla*	*(12)*
1	*teaspoon almond extract*	*(8)*
¼	*cup skimmed milk*	*(22)*
1½	*cups sifted flour*	*(627)*
4	*ounces almonds (about 1 cup) freshly ground*	*(680)*

1. Cream the butter and sugar together until light and fluffy. Add the vanilla, almond extract, and milk and beat again. Resift the flour and gradually work it into the creamed batter. Add the almonds and when they are completely incorporated, knead the

dough for a few minutes to blend all the ingredients thoroughly. Pat into a smooth ball, place on a dish, cover, and refrigerate for at least ½ hour.

Preheat oven to 325°.

2. Take a generous teaspoon of the chilled dough and work it between your palms to form a small roll; blend it into a crescent shape as you place it on an ungreased cookie sheet. Bake for 12 to 15 minutes, or just until the crescents turn a sandy color. Do not overbake.

❊ Fudge Brownies

total calories — 1459 • per brownie — 46

The calorie count on regular store-bought brownies will be only 10 to 15 points higher than this recipe. (And consider what you are buying — a lot of preservatives and artificial flavor, which we can all do without.) But comparing the Fudge Brownies in this recipe with those usually made at home is another matter: 45 calories versus 150–180. Now that's a *big* difference. A large part of the disparity is accounted for by the amount of butter used. Here butter adds flavor and minimal fat. What is missing is the longer storage life of the brownies. They must be kept in an airtight container, for after two or three days they tend to dry out. However, these Fudge Brownies are very easy to make, so a pan of them can be whipped together whenever there is a craving.

Makes 32 1 × 2–inch brownies

1	ounce unsweetened chocolate	(135)
1	tablespoon water or coffee	——
4	tablespoons butter	(408)
2	eggs	(154)
3	tablespoons sugar	(138)
2	teaspoons vanilla	(12)
1	cup sifted cake flour	(349)
½	teaspoon baking powder	(3)
½	teaspoon salt	——
⅓	cup walnuts, chopped into coarse bits	(260)

Preheat oven to 350°.

1. In a small pot over low heat, melt together the chocolate, water or coffee, and butter. Meanwhile beat together in a bowl the eggs and sugar until light and fluffy. Add the sugar, a tablespoon at a time, beating thoroughly between each addition. Add the vanilla, scrape in the melted chocolate mixture, and beat well.

2. Resift the flour with the baking powder and salt and stir it into the chocolate batter. Finally, stir in the nuts. Select an 8 × 8-inch nonstick baking pan, or lightly grease a regular pan. Scrape the batter into the pan and smooth out with a spatula. Bake for 15 minutes. Remove from the oven and cool.

3. Cut rectangles by slicing the Fudge Brownie into four equal strips in one direction and eight in the other direction. Keep the brownies in an airtight container.

❀ Butterscotch Brownies

total calories — 1275 • per brownie — 40

Brownies are usually thought of as dark bars of chocolate flavor. For a change of pace, try these Butterscotch Brownies that bake to a warm caramel color and contain a cool calorie count by limiting the fat.

Makes 32 1 × 2–inch brownies

¾ cup dark brown sugar	(408)
3 tablespoons oil	(360)
1 tablespoon maple syrup	(50)
2 teaspoons vanilla	(12)
¾ cup flour	(336)
1 teaspoon baking powder	(5)
½ teaspoon salt	——
2 tablespoons walnuts, chopped into coarse bits	(104)

Preheat oven to 350°.

1. Stir together the brown sugar, oil, maple syrup, and vanilla. Measure the flour, baking powder, and salt into a sifter and

gradually sift the dry ingredients into the bowl, blending well between each addition. Finally, stir in the nuts.

2. Select an 8 × 8–inch nonstick cake pan or lightly grease a regular pan. Spoon the batter into the pan and bake about 20 minutes, or until a toothpick plunged in the center comes out clean. Remove from the oven and cool for 15 minutes.

3. Slice the brownies in four equal strips in one direction, then in eight equal strips in the other.

✿ Graham Cracker Brownie Bars

total calories — 1479 • per bar — 31

Substituting graham cracker crumbs for flour gives the brownies a special flavor. That switch also saves about 5 calories per brownie.

Makes 48 1 × 1½–inch bars

2	cups graham cracker crumbs	(652)
¼	cup sugar	(192)
¼	teaspoon salt	——
1	cup skimmed milk	(88)
⅓	cup walnuts, chopped	(260)
⅓	cup semisweet chocolate bits	(287)

Preheat oven to 350°.

1. Stir together in a mixing bowl the crumbs, sugar, and salt. Pour in the milk and stir until it is thoroughly blended with the dry ingredients. Finally, mix in the walnuts and chocolate bits.

2. Scrape the batter into a 9 × 9–inch nonstick baking pan or a lightly greased regular pan. Bake for about 30 minutes. Cool for 10 minutes, then cut into six equal strips in one direction and eight strips in the other.

❀ Meringue Puffs

total calories — 633 • per meringue — 25

Meringue puffs can be stubborn and refuse to stay puffed, especially when the sugar has been cut almost in half, as in this recipe. To assure perfect results every time, the preparation method must be changed. For this reason I use the Italian meringue principle and precook the egg whites and sugar, much as in a fondant.

Makes about 25 1½-inch puffs

2	egg whites	(30)
¾	cups sugar	(577)
¼	teaspoon cream of tartar	——
⅓	cup cold water	——
1	tablespoon vanilla	(18)
1	teaspoon almond extract	(8)

Preheat oven to 325°.

1. Line a baking sheet with parchment paper, or use an unlined nonstick cookie sheet. In the top of a double boiler (or in an ordinary, but heavy, pot placed on a heat-deflector pad), combine all the ingredients except the vanilla and almond extract. Mix well for a minute off the heat with an electric beater at low speed.

2. Place the pot on the heat and continue beating at medium speed for about 10 minutes, or until the mixture is quite firm and holds its shape. Occasionally give a burst of high speed while beating. Remove from the heat, add vanilla and almond extract, and continue beating at high speed for another minute.

3. Use a pastry bag or two teaspoons for forming the puffs. Allow a heaping teaspoon per puff and leave about a ¾-inch space between the meringues. Bake for about 1 hour, or until the meringues lift easily from the sheet and are dry and crisp to the touch. Once cool, keep in an airtight container.

❈ Cottage Cheese Sweet Snack

calories per serving with cracker — 60 • with toast — 65

Cooks have constant need for an individual dessert that can be put together quickly. Here is a very handy and unusual one to keep in mind. Not only is it a light mealtime finish, but can be a surprising, and filling, midday bite as well.

Serves 1

1	tablespoon low-fat cottage cheese	(8)
1½	teaspoons part skim-milk ricotta	(11)
¼	teaspoon sugar	(4)
	pinch of cinnamon	——
	pinch of nutmeg	——
¼	teaspoon vanilla	(2)
1	4-inch round soda or cream cracker,	(35)
	or 1 slice melba-thin white bread, toasted	(40)

Mix all the ingredients except the cracker together in a small bowl. Spread the mixture on the cracker or toast, making certain that the topping reaches to the edges. Place on a piece of aluminum foil on the broiler rack. Heat under the broiler until the cheese bubbles. Serve at once.

❈ Chocolate Thins

total calories — 450 • per chocolate — 20

Don't look for much chocolate in this book. It's far too rich for dieting purposes, but since it is so good, here is a thin way around the agonizing dilemma. Pure chocolate is used, but is stretched thin, thin, thin so that the number of calories put on the plate are incredibly few. A single wafer served on a chilled dish makes a very understated and elegant dessert.

Makes about 22 1½-inch chocolates

3 ounces sweet chocolate   *(450)*
  cookie sheet
  wax paper
2 rubber spatulas
  cookie cutters

1. Timing is important, so select and arrange all equipment. Choose a cookie sheet that will fit into the freezer and line it with wax paper. Pick out from your assortment of cookie cutters all those that measure about 1½ inches in diameter. One cutter will be needed for each chocolate — thus 22 are required for the full recipe — but a half can be done at a time. Place the cookie forms near the baking sheet. Have two rubber spatulas handy.

2. Break the chocolate into pieces as you place it in a small, heavy pot. Add nothing else. Turn the heat to low and slowly melt the chocolate, stirring from time to time with a wooden spatula. As soon as the chocolate is melted, pour it onto the wax paper, scraping the pot clean with a spatula. Spread the melted chocolate into a thin layer with the rubber spatula, then clean off the first spatula with the second. Every bit of chocolate counts. Work quickly. Firmly press the cookie cutters into the chocolate and leave them in place. Arrange the forms as close together as possible. Put the cookie sheet into the freezer for about 2 minutes, or until the chocolate loses its shine and takes on a dull look.

3. One by one, remove the cookie cutters from the wax paper. This is facilitated by reaching under the paper with your other hand and breaking the solid chocolate around each form. Gently press the cookie form with the palms of your hands; the heat will help release the chocolate shapes. Place them in a plastic container, cover, and put in the freezer.

4. With a sharp knife, lift from the wax paper all the unused chocolate; remelt. Repeat the process, relining the cookie sheet with fresh wax paper. It is unlikely that more than one remelting will be necessary. The chocolates should remain in the freezer or the coldest part of the refrigerator until served. Present the underside of the wafer up, because it will be smoother than the top.

❀ Pies

As AMERICAN as apple pie, the old saying goes, probably in reference to mother's legendary specialty. But today it's a less-fattening apple pie that we are seeking. Several are included in this chapter, as well as chocolate, peach, orange, pineapple, and pumpkin pies, and that great French classic, the individual strawberry tart.

Pies present a dilemma to the calorie-wary. Even though the filling might be light, the pastry, by its very nature, isn't. A special pastry has been developed for this book that trims away half the usual number of calories in homemade crusts. I think this recipe stands out from other low-calorie doughs in that the crust has flavor and is tender and flaky. Even so, in most instances its 746 calories for the entire crust add up to more than the filling it contains — obviously, the more pie crust left on the plate, the better. The graham cracker and ginger snap crusts have fewer still, but I don't find them suitable for all pies.

❀ Apple Meringue Tart

*total calories in filling — 766 • pie shell — 746
calories per serving — 151*

Whole chunks of cooked apples nestle beneath the crunchy meringue topping, providing a pleasant change from the usual custard-smooth fillings. By using the same sugar twice — once

143

to cook the apples and again in the meringue — many, many calories are saved. One final surprise — a scattering of ground almonds in the meringue.

Serves 10

½ cup sugar	(385)
¼ cup water	——
3 apples (about 1 lb.)	(245)
1 deep 9-inch pie shell, prebaked (page 158)	
3 egg whites, room temperature	(45)
pinch of cream of tartar	——
1 teaspoon vanilla	(6)
½ ounce almonds, freshly ground (about 2½ tablespoons)	(85)

1. Pour the sugar and water into a wide pot or skillet, put on medium heat, cover, and bring to a simmer. Meanwhile, peel the apples, cut into eighths lengthwise, and core. Add the apples to the boiling syrup, re-cover, and cook until the fruit is soft but not mushy, about 5 to 7 minutes. Once or twice during the cooking, carefully turn the apples, using two wooden spoons to prevent breaking them. With a slotted spoon, lift the cooked apples onto paper towels; let them drain thoroughly. If the pot is too large to pour from easily later on, transfer the syrup to a smaller pot. When the apples have cooled, arrange them in the bottom of the prebaked pie shell.

Preheat the oven to 325°.

2. Place the reserved syrup on medium heat and bring to the boiling point while beating the egg whites sprinkled with cream of tartar. When the whites are quite firm and the syrup has boiled for about 5 minutes, pour the syrup over the beaten whites while continuing to beat at medium speed. Then add the vanilla and beat at high speed until the meringue is completely cool. Carefully fold in the ground almonds.

3. Spoon the beaten whites over the apples and use a rubber spatula to smooth them into a topping that reaches all the way to the crust rim. If desired, slash through the meringue in a few places to allow the apples to show through. Place in the oven for 15 to 20 minutes, or until the meringue is a nice golden color. Remove and cool.

�֍ Vermont Apple Pie

total calories in filling — 935 • pie shell — 746
calories per serving — 168

This applesauce filling has a custardlike consistency, but one with plenty of body. In the summer, when apples are not at their best, use a good brand of natural, unsweetened applesauce to fill the shell. The garnishing apple is greatly improved by a coating of freshly made caramel.

Serves 10

2½ cups (20 ounces) unsweetened applesauce	(250)
2 tablespoons brown sugar	(68)
rind 1 lemon, grated	——
1 tablespoon lemon juice	(4)
½ teaspoon cinnamon	(3)
½ teaspoon nutmeg	(6)
1 tablespoon butter, melted and cooled	(102)
1 egg	(77)
3 tablespoons cornstarch	(87)
1 9-inch pie shell, unbaked (page 158)	
1 medium apple, peeled, quartered, and cored	(53)
2 tablespoons granulated sugar (for poaching)	(92)
½ cup granulated sugar (for caramelizing)	(193)*
½ cup plus 2 tablespoons water	——

Preheat oven to 375°.

1. Put the applesauce into a mixing bowl, sprinkle on the brown sugar, lemon rind, lemon juice, cinnamon, and nutmeg and beat well with a whisk. Stir together in a small bowl the melted butter and egg and add the cornstarch; beat until very smooth, then scrape into the applesauce and mix well. Pour this filling into the pie shell and bake for about 30 minutes, or until a knife inserted in the center comes out clean. Cool.

2. Make a poaching syrup by boiling together ½ cup of water with 2 tablespoons of granulated sugar. Simmer for 5 minutes,

* Less than half of the caramel will be eaten (see Step 3).

then add the quartered apple, cover, and cook until the apples are soft but still slightly firm, about 5 to 8 minutes, depending on the fruit. Lift the apples out of the syrup and drain on paper towels. When they are thoroughly drained, cut into thick slices and place around the outer edge of the pie.

3. Put the remaining ½ cup of granulated sugar in a small, heavy pot, sprinkle on 2 tablespoons of water, and place on moderately high heat to caramelize. Watch the caramel carefully; once it becomes dark brown it can turn to burnt sugar in an instant. Work quickly now. With a pastry brush, paint each apple slice with the hot caramel, then go over them one more time. Place the caramelized apples around the outer edge of the pie. (Note: Even though less than half the caramel will be used, working with a smaller quantity would present a problem by cooling too quickly. The remaining caramel can be cleaned from the pan by filling with hot water once the pan has cooled, then boiling rapidly.)

✿ Chocolate Pie

total calories in filling — 806 • pie shell — 746
calories per serving —194

The full chocolate flavor of this pie is achieved by combining a minimal amount of the real stuff with a more substantial proportion of cocoa, which is low in calories. Not only does the one ounce of chocolate add richness, but it also helps firm the filling.

Serves 8

1	ounce semisweet chocolate	(144)
2	teaspoons rum	(8)
1½	cups skimmed milk	(132)
1	egg	(77)
3	tablespoons cornstarch	(87)
¼	cup cocoa	(56)
½	cup evaporated skimmed milk	(96)
2	tablespoons sugar	(92)

1   tablespoon butter   (102)
2   teaspoons vanilla   (12)
1   8-inch pie shell, prebaked (page 158)
    Optional: meringue topping (page 202)

1. Chop the chocolate into several pieces and place them in a small pot with the rum and ¼ cup of the skimmed milk. Put the pot on very low heat to melt the chocolate.

2. Meanwhile, in a heavy nonaluminum pot beat the egg. Add the cornstarch, a tablespoon at a time, and beat until smooth. A wire whisk works best for this. Sprinkle on the cocoa and continue beating, then stir in the remaining 1¼ cups of skimmed milk and the evaporated skimmed milk.

3. Scrape in the melted chocolate, add the sugar, and place the pot on medium heat while whisking constantly so that the mixture does not boil. When the liquid becomes quite thick, remove the pot from the fire and stir in the butter and vanilla. Cool the filling for about 5 minutes and spoon into the pie shell. Cool completely, then chill. (If the optional meringue topping is used, bake it while the filling is still warm.)

❀ Orange Custard Pie

total calories for filling — 520 • pie shell — 746
calories per serving — 158

Good, fresh orange flavor is not used in pies often enough. Both the color and taste are bright and sunny. Here that taste is intensified by cooking the orange slices with the rinds, thus capturing all of the pungent oils for the sauce. The rinds soften and sweeten during the cooking and are deliciously edible. Cream has been eliminated from the custard to bring the calorie count to a light 65 per portion. The more pastry left on the plate the better.

Serves 8

1	*large navel orange*	*(71)*
1	*cup orange juice*	*(110)*
1	*tablespoon orange liqueur*	*(12)*
¼	*cup sugar*	*(192)*
1	*egg*	*(77)*
2	*tablespoons cornstarch*	*(58)*
¼	*teaspoon salt*	———
1	*8-inch pie shell, prebaked (page 158)*	

1. Cut the unpeeled orange into thin slices and place them in a saucepan. Pour the orange juice, liqueur, and sugar over the oranges. Bring the liquid to the boiling point, reduce heat, cover, and simmer for 20 minutes.

2. Lift the orange slices out of the syrup and put them in a sieve that is suspended over a bowl. Allow the slices to drain for at least 15 minutes.

3. With a whisk, beat the egg in a heavy saucepan. Sprinkle on the cornstarch, a tablespoon at a time, and beat well until the egg and cornstarch are smoothly blended. Add the salt, then pour in the cooking syrup in a thin stream while beating with the whisk. Add the drained syrup from the orange slices. Place the pan over medium heat and stir with the whisk until the sauce thickens, about 5 minutes. Do not allow the sauce to boil. Cool a little.

4. Spread the filling in the bottom of the pie shell. Smooth the surface with a rubber spatula and decorate with the orange slices arranged in an overlapping ring. Chill.

❈ Pear Custard Pie

total calories in filling — 481–514 • pie shell — 746
calories per serving — 153–158

Although canned pears can be used for this refreshingly delicate pie, taste and texture will not be the same as when fresh fruit is used. Canned pears are usually overprocessed to an almost mushy stage and can never approximate the tang of the fresh fruit. However, if canned pears are used, make certain they are not packed in sweetened syrup, and please do not substitute the packing liquid for pear nectar. Which brings up a point about current marketing practices that make it necessary to read labels carefully. After one surprisingly bland testing of this recipe I noticed that the first ingredient listed on the pear juice can was water, which meant I was working with more water than juice. If your local supermarket does not carry pure fruit nectars, try a Latin specialty store.

Serves 8

1 to 1¼ cups pear nectar	*(130–163)*
1 tablespoon kirsch	*(12)*
2 tablespoons sugar	*(92)*
1 medium pear, preferably Bartlett	*(95)*
1 egg	*(77)*
2 tablespoons cornstarch	*(58)*
¼ teaspoon salt	——
1 8-inch pie shell, prebaked (page 158)	
1 teaspoon red jelly — currant or raspberry	*(17)*

1. Select a pan or skillet that will hold the pear sections in one layer. Pour in 1 cup of pear nectar, the kirsch, and the sugar; bring this liquid to a boil, cover, reduce heat, and simmer slowly while preparing the pear.

2. Peel the pear, cut it in eighths, core, and slip the pieces into the syrup. Re-cover and cook until the fruit sections are soft but not overcooked. To prevent bruising the pears, use two wooden spoons to turn the sections carefully once or twice during the cooking period. Keep in mind that the hot fruit will soften a little more after being removed from the cooking syrup. Lift the pears out of the syrup with a skimmer and put them in a sieve that is suspended over a bowl. Allow the pears to drain for at least 15 minutes.

3. With a whisk, beat the egg in a heavy saucepan. Sprinkle on the cornstarch, a tablespoon at a time, and beat well until the egg and cornstarch are smoothly blended. Measure the cooking syrup and fill out to 1 cup with extra pear nectar if necessary. Add the

salt to the egg base, then pour in the liquid in a thin stream while beating with the whisk. Add the drained syrup from the pears. Place the pan over medium heat and stir with the whisk until the sauce thickens, about 5 minutes. Do not allow the sauce to boil. Cool slightly, then spread the filling in the bottom of the pie shell. Smooth the surface with a rubber spatula and decorate with the pear sections arranged in a wheelspoke pattern. Chill.

4. In a butter melter or similar small pot, dissolve the jelly over very low heat, stirring with a spoon a few times. Cool the jelly for a minute or two, then paint onto the surface of the pie with a pastry brush. Chill to set the jelly and remove to a cool spot.

❦ Mocha Ricotta Pie

total calories in filling — 503 • pie shell — 746
calories per serving — 156

Creamy in texture but mercifully moderate in calories, ricotta cheese beautifully absorbs many flavorings, in this case coffee and cocoa. The finished pie has a delicate air about it that the first taste affirms.

Serves 8

1¼ cups water	——
1 tablespoon gelatin	(23)
1 tablespoon plus 1 teaspoon cocoa	(19)
1 tablespoon instant coffee, preferably freeze-dried	(5)
2 tablespoons sugar	(92)
1 teaspoon amaretto	(4)
1 cup (½ pound) part skim-milk ricotta cheese	(360)
1 8-inch pie shell, prebaked (page 158)	

1. Pour ¼ cup water into a small bowl or cup and sprinkle on the gelatin; put the remaining cup of water in a small pot and bring to a boil. Meanwhile, measure 1 tablespoon of the cocoa, the instant coffee, sugar, and amaretto into a mixing bowl, pour on the boiling water, and stir briefly. Immediately scoop in the softened gelatin and stir until it has completely dissolved. Put aside to cool.

2. Pour the mocha mixture into the blender and with the motor running, add the ricotta cheese, a heaping tablespoon at a time. After all the ingredients have been thoroughly blended, give a final burst at high speed.

3. Pour the mocha mixture into the baked pie shell and refrigerate until the filling sets. Remove the pie from the refrigerator about 30 minutes before serving. Just before serving, put the remaining teaspoon of cocoa in a small sieve and shake it over the surface of the pie.

❧ Blueberry Pie

total calories in filling — 443 • pie shell — 746
calories per serving – 149

At the height of the blueberry season the fruit will be somewhat sweeter than the early crops. Taste for sugar before adding the amount indicated below, you might be able to do with less. On the other hand, out of season, when frozen unsweetened berries are used, all the sugar will be needed.

Serves 8

2	cups blueberries	(180)
1¼	cups water	——
¼	cup sugar	(192)
¼	teaspoon nutmeg	(3)
1	tablespoon cornstarch	(29)
1	tablespoon kirsch	(12)
1	tablespoon lemon juice	(4)
1	tablespoon gelatin	(23)
1	9-inch pie shell, prebaked (page 158)	

1. Pick the stems off the blueberries; if frozen berries are used, measure them without thawing and rinse. Put the berries in a saucepot, add 1 cup water, the sugar, and nutmeg. In a small bowl mix together the cornstarch, kirsch, and lemon juice and stir this paste into the blueberries. Place the pot on medium heat and slowly bring to the boiling point; simmer for 5 minutes while

stirring. The thickened sauce should turn from opaque to translucent during this time.

2. While the berries are cooking, soften the gelatin in the remaining ¼ cup of water. As soon as the pot is taken off the heat, scoop in the gelatin and stir until it is completely dissolved. Cool the filling, pour it into the pie shell, and refrigerate to set the gelatin. Remove from the refrigerator about 30 minutes before serving.

✿ Pineapple Pie

total calories in filling — 834 • *pie shell — 746*
calories per serving — 198

Delicious pineapple is one of nature's strongly flavored fruits that is best left pure. No exotic additions are necessary, just a little help to turn crushed pineapple into a light and sunny open-face pie.

Serves 8

3	tablespoons cornstarch	(87)
¼	teaspoon salt	——
¼	cup sugar	(192)
2	eggs, beaten	(154)
1	20-ounce can unsweetened crushed pineapple	(350)
1	8-inch pie shell, prebaked (page 158)	
1	tablespoon jelly, guava or currant	(51)

1. In a heavy enameled or stainless-steel pot, mix together the cornstarch, salt, and sugar. Stir in the eggs, then the pineapple with its juice, and place the pot on medium heat. Stir while cooking until the pie filling thickens and the liquid turns slightly transparent, about 5 to 8 minutes; do not allow the mixture to boil. Remove the pot from the heat and cool the filling slightly.

2. Scrape the filling into the baked pie shell and smooth the top with a rubber spatula. Cool, then chill in the refrigerator.

3. In a very small pot or butter melter, dissolve the jelly over

very low heat while stirring constantly. Cool the jelly a few minutes, then paint it over the surface of the chilled pie. Replace the pie in the refrigerator to set the jelly glaze quickly, then remove to a cool spot.

✿ Glazed Peach Pie

total calories in filling — 459 • crumb crust — 557
calories per serving — 127

When fresh peaches are in season cooks look for a variety of ways to serve them. Here is an easy-to-do possibility, and one that lets the natural flavor of the fruit dominate.

Serves 8

3 cups sliced peaches (4 or 5)	(195)
2 tablespoons sugar	(92)
1 tablespoon lemon juice	(4)
½ cup water	—
2 tablespoons gelatin	(46)
1 cup orange juice	(110)
1 tablespoon orange liqueur	(12)
1 9-inch Graham Cracker Crust (page 159)	

1. Peel the peaches and cut into slices about ¼ inch thick. Work over a bowl to catch any dripping juices. Place the slices in a bowl and sprinkle over them the sugar and lemon juice, then mix with your hands to coat all the peach slices with the sugar. Cover and put aside.

2. Put the water in a small bowl and sprinkle on the gelatin; put aside to soften. Meanwhile, pour the orange juice and liqueur into a small pot and bring to a boil. Take the pot off the heat and stir in the softened gelatin. Remove ½ cup of the syrup and reserve. Cool the remaining syrup.

3. Taste the peach juices and if not sweet enough, add a little extra sugar. Pour the cooled syrup over the peaches and mix well; again, your hands make the best implement. Refrigerate the peaches until the syrup begins to jell.

4. Spoon the peaches and their jelly into the pie shell and pat the surface to smooth it. Refrigerate until quite firm. Pour on the reserved syrup and return to the refrigerator until it sets into a clear glaze on top.

❊ Glazed Strawberry Pie

total calories in filling — 591 • pie shell — 746
calories per serving — 167

Thanks to rapid transportation, the strawberry season is getting longer and longer. Its prolonged availability means cooks have more chance to treat the noble berry in new ways. This glazed pie is definitely one to try at the next opportunity. It is a double strawberry presentation — first sliced and layered in the pie shell, then cooked as a custard to fill the shell. In fact, the only disturbing note I find in this recipe is mashing the beautiful fresh berries. The final taste, though, is reward for such ravaging.

Serves 8

    1 baked 8-inch pie shell *(page 158)*
    2 cups Strawberry Filling *(page 193)*   *(481)*
    2 cups strawberries   *(110)*
        Optional: Whipped Topping *(page 203)*

1. Bake the pie shell and prepare the Strawberry Filling; cool both. Slice the whole berries in half and place in the bottom of the pie shell, cut side down. Reserve a few berries to decorate the top, if you wish. Spoon the filling over the berries and smooth the top nicely. Chill.
2. If using the optional Whipped Topping, spread it over the top of the pie at serving time, but leave clear a large circle in the center. The contrast between the bright red filling and white topping is most attractive. Decorate with the reserved whole berries, if desired, by placing them in the center.

❀ Strawberry Tarts

total calories — 1323   •   per tart — 221

No French pastry display would be complete without fresh fruit tarts, particularly strawberry. Each individual tart holds a thin layer of pale cream sauce crowned with several berries shining with glaze. Those tarts can be devilishly rich (about 450 calories each), but need not be. All three components in this recipe have been carefully prepared to trim away superfluous calories without sacrificing taste. Individual tarts demand a little more time to prepare than a pie but are well worth the effort. Few dessert temptations are so festive and pretty.

Serves 6

1	*Pastry Dough recipe (page 158)*	*(746)*
1	*cup Vanilla Pastry Cream (page 192)*	*(384)*
18	*strawberries, rinsed, hulled, and dried*	*(90)*
2	*tablespoons fruit jelly — currant, raspberry, or*	
	strawberry	*(102)*
¼	*teaspoon orange liqueur*	*(1)*

Preheat oven to 375°.

1. Roll out the pastry dough and cut into 6 4-inch rounds. Fit the pastry into 6 individual 3½-inch tart pans, pushing the dough into the fluted sides so they will take on that form. Also push the dough lightly upward a little to create a deeper shell. Prick each shell bottom with a small, sharp knife. Place parchment paper in each tart pan and fill with dry beans or other weights. Bake for 10 minutes, or until the edges begin to brown slightly. Remove from the oven, scoop out the beans, discard the paper, prick the shells again in one or two places, and return them to the oven. Turn off the heat and finish baking the shells for another 5 minutes. Remove from the oven and cool.

2. Meanwhile, prepare the Vanilla Pastry Cream, flavoring with vanilla and orange liqueur. Put aside to cool.

3. Spoon 3 tablespoons of the pastry cream into each shell while melting the fruit jelly with ¼ teaspoon orange liqueur in a small pot or butter melter. Allow the glaze to cool for a few min-

utes before using it to glaze the strawberries. One by one, paint the berries by lightly piercing the stem end on the tines of a two-pronged confectioners' fork or any small fork. With a pastry brush, paint the entire surface of each berry, immediately placing the glazed fruit onto the pastry cream, stem side down. Arrange 3 berries in a small circle in the center of each tart. Cool completely.

4. To serve: Arrange the tarts on a round serving platter or present them on individual dessert dishes along with a fork and spoon.

❀ Pumpkin Chiffon Pie

total calories in filling — 383 • crumb crust — 585
calories per serving — 161

Pumpkin pie, whether chiffon, frozen, or regular is a long-standing American favorite. It is presented here with all its good flavor intact. Some of the sweetness is missing, but not so you'd notice.

Serves 6

¼	cup orange juice	(27)
1	tablespoon gelatin	(23)
1	cup cooked pumpkin	(81)
1	egg yolk, 2 egg whites, room temperature	(92)
1	tablespoon dark corn syrup	(60)
2	tablespoons brown sugar	(68)
¼	cup skimmed milk	(22)
¼	teaspoon each cinnamon, nutmeg, ginger	(7)
½	teaspoon vanilla	(3)
	pinch of cream of tartar	——
1	8-inch Ginger Snap Crust (page 160)	

1. Pour the orange juice into a small bowl or cup and sprinkle the gelatin over it. Meanwhile, in a 6- to 8-cup heavy pot stir together the pumpkin, egg yolk, corn syrup, brown sugar, skimmed milk, spices, and vanilla. Put the pot over medium heat and stir

while cooking for about 2 minutes. Remove the pot from the fire, scrape in the softened gelatin, and stir until it is dissolved.

2. Beat the egg whites with the cream of tartar until firm. Spoon about one-third of the beaten whites over the hot pumpkin and fold in thoroughly. Scrape in the rest of the whites and carefully fold them in just until evenly distributed. Do not overwork the whites.

3. Pour the filling into the prepared pie shell and place in the refrigerator to set the gelatin quickly. Once the filling is firm, the pie can be removed from the refrigerator and kept in a cool spot.

❀ Pastry Dough

total calories — 746

It seemed like a contradiction in terms — a really good low-calorie pastry dough — and I feared it could not be done. I believe it has. Not only does this pastry have excellent flavor, it is also tender. Much trial and error led to two basic changes that did the trick: No water is added and one egg replaces most of the fat. The net result is 746 calories versus about 1600 for regular homemade pastry. Do follow the directions exactly, however. Every calorie has been counted, so use them all. Until I scraped the residual melted butter and egg out of the cup before working the dough with my fingers, it was a little dry. Those few extra drops, which can be as much as a teaspoon, count. Eggs, of course, vary in size, and flours differ as well, but basically no changes in quantities should be necessary. Regular all-purpose flour and a medium-sized egg were used in the testing. I also found that the pastry worked better with another departure from the usual technique: The dough is best used shortly after being made. It can be used immediately, but a 15-minute rest period — during which it should not be refrigerated — is beneficial. If made in advance, however, it must be kept cold because of the raw egg in the recipe. After being chilled the dough will not be quite so tender. Once you read how quickly and easily the pastry can be stirred together, you can relax and make it on the spur of the moment.

157

Makes 1 single 8- or 9-inch pie shell or 6 3½-inch tart shells

1 cup sifted flour	(419)
¼ teaspoon salt	——
1 tablespoon sugar	(46)
1 medium egg, room temperature	(77)
2 tablespoons butter, melted and cooled	(204)

1. Place the sifted flour in a mixing bowl and stir in the salt and sugar. Beat the egg in a small bowl or cup, then add the melted butter and beat again. Stir this egg-and-butter mixture into the flour, mixing with a fork until the flour is absorbed by the liquid. Moisten your fingers by scraping them around the inside of the bowl used for the egg and butter. Work the dough lightly with your moistened fingers until it forms a ball. No water should be necessary, but if you find the dough too dry, add only the amount of water absolutely necessary to make the pastry hold together in a ball.

2. Lightly flour the working surface and with the heel of your hand push small sections of the dough away from you, pushing them about 6 inches. Reassemble the dough and repeat the process. This thoroughly blends the fat and flour together. Reform the dough into a smooth ball, cover with wax paper, and rest the dough for 15 minutes, but do not refrigerate.

3. If a recipe calls for a prebaked pie shell, preheat the oven to 375°. Roll out the dough, fit it into the pie dish, and flute the edges. Prick the bottom of the pie shell with a fork or a small, sharp knife, fit a sheet of parchment paper (or, lacking parchment paper, wax paper) over the pastry, and weight with dry beans, rice, marbles, or manufactured pie weights. Another possible method is to place a slightly smaller pie dish over the paper, but unless the second dish presses against the sides of the dough, this doesn't work as well. Bake for 10 to 15 minutes, or until the crust is firm, opaque, and lightly colored. To avoid a soggy bottom I also suggest that you remove the weights and paper from the pie dish, prick the bottom of the shell again, and return to the oven, with heat turned off, to finish baking the bottom for about 5 minutes.

❀ Graham Cracker Crust

total calories — 557

Even though the pie crust that uses regular flour on page 158 is only half as caloric as most recipes, almost 200 additional calories are trimmed when graham cracker crumbs replace the flour.

Makes 1 8-inch pie shell

1 tablespoon butter	*(102)*
1 cup graham cracker crumbs	*(326)*
1 teaspoon cinnamon	*(6)*
1 tablespoon sugar	*(46)*
1 egg	*(77)*

Preheat oven to 350°.

1. Melt the butter and put aside to cool. Pour the crumbs into a mixing bowl, add the cinnamon and sugar, and stir to distribute the flavorings. Lightly beat the egg, add the melted butter, and stir into the crumbs.

2. Pat the moistened crumbs into an 8-inch pie dish. If you encounter any problem with the crumbs sticking to your fingers, use a piece of plastic wrap for patting the crumbs into place. Bake for about 10 minutes to set the crust.

❀ Ginger Snap Crust

total calories — 585

A few extra calories are sacrificed in this crumb crust as compared to the Graham Cracker Crust in the preceding recipe. Still, there are times when the extra zip of the ginger flavor marries perfectly with the filling — pumpkin chiffon for one.

Makes 1 8-inch pie shell

3	ounces ginger snaps (about 15 1¾-inch snaps)	(357)
1	tablespoon butter	(102)
½	teaspoon cinnamon	(3)
1	tablespoon sugar	(46)
1	egg	(77)

Preheat oven to 350°.

1. Crush the ginger snaps into fine crumbs; an electric blender or food processor makes fast work of this. The snaps can also be put in a brown paper bag and crushed with a rolling pin.

2. Follow the directions for Graham Cracker Crust in the preceding recipe.

❀ Cakes and Pastries

F LOUR-BASED DESSERTS are the real bugaboos among low-
calorie desserts. A single cup of unsifted all-purpose flour is a
brimming 455 calories. And since that is only the beginning and
contains no flavors, much that is good and rich has to be added
if something tempting is to be created. There are several avenues
open to the diet-minded cook: substituting less-rich ingredients
that still carry a lot of flavor, stretching wherever possible with
fruits to provide extra portions, and streamlining pastry classics.
Specifically, an old-fashioned apple turnover evolved into Apples
in Gilded Cages, in which a whole apple is encased in a few strips
of pastry, saving as much as 150 calories in the process.

Nonstick cake pans are, of course, a necessity for low-calorie
baking. If you must bake without them, consider greasing the
pans with mineral oil rather than vegetable oil or butter. Mineral
oil has no flavor, contains no calories at all, and does a superb
greasing job. When it is used in such a negligible quantity one
needn't be concerned about its laxative effect. It hasn't affected
my friends or family that way.

Cutting wax paper to fit a round cake pan is easy and accurate
if done this way: Tear off a sheet of wax paper larger than the
cake pan; fold it in half and continue folding in half lengthwise
until it is reduced to a sharp-edged triangle about ¾ inches wide
at the bottom. Holding the triangle horizontal, place the sharp
point on the center of the bottom of the pan and cut the paper
at the rim. Open up the paper and it is perfectly round and perfectly sized to the pan.

161

❊ Angel Food Cake

total calories — 1285 • per serving — 107

The beauty of Angel Food Cake as a low-calorie dessert is that there is not a trace of fat in it, not even to grease the pan. In fact, if any fat were accidentally included, the whole gorgeous confection would be ruined. In most recipes for the cake at least 1½ cups of sugar are called for. I have experimented in bringing down that lavish quantity and find that an entire half-cupful can be dispensed with, saving almost 400 calories. The procedure is exact, but not difficult. An electric mixer or electric hand-beater helps considerably.

Angel Food Cake can be dusted with confectioners' sugar and served plain, or accompanied by sliced fresh strawberries or other fruits in season. Low-calorie icings can be found in the chapter on icings and fillings. Particularly felicitous is Orange Glaze (page 199); only ¾ cup will ice the top and sides of the cake, adding only 25 calories per serving.

Serves 12

1	cup sifted cake flour	(349)
½	teaspoon salt	——
1	cup sugar	(770)
1¼	cups egg whites (about 10 eggs), room temperature	(150)
1	teaspoon cream of tartar	(2)
1	tablespoon warm water	——
1	tablespoon lemon juice, room temperature	(4)
1	teaspoon vanilla	(6)
½	teaspoon almond extract	(4)

Preheat oven to 350°.

1. Combine the sifted flour with the salt and ¼ cup of sugar and resift 4 times, holding the sifter high above the bowl to incorporate as much air as possible. Sift the remaining ¾ cup sugar into another dish or bowl.

2. Start beating the egg whites and when they are foamy, add the cream of tartar. Beat another half-minute, then add the water and lemon juice and beat until the whites are stiff but not dry.

3. Begin adding the sifted sugar a tablespoon at a time while continuing to beat. Each addition must be thoroughly dissolved before more sugar is put in. After all the sugar has been incorporated, beat in the vanilla and almond extract.

4. Sift about ¼ of the flour-and-sugar mixture over the beaten whites, then fold in lightly and carefully with a rubber spatula. Continue gradually sifting and folding in the remaining dry ingredients.

5. Carefully spoon the batter into an ungreased 9- or 10-inch tube pan. Smooth the surface lightly with the rubber spatula. With a stainless-steel or silver knife, cut through the batter in a circle to eliminate any air pockets. Place in the oven for 40 to 45 minutes, or until the top is a dark golden color and the cake springs back when pressed. Remove from the oven and cool upside down. Some angel food pans have feet on them for this purpose, which raise the pan enough to keep air circulating around the cake. Lacking such a pan, invert the tube on a bottle, funnel, or glass, or place on a cake rack. Allow the cake to cool for about 2 hours.

6. To remove the cake from the pan, use a sharp, thin knife to cut around the outside edge and the center tube. Push the detachable bottom upward and lift the cake away. Carefully cut the cake loose from the metal bottom.

7. To serve: Do not use a knife to cut the cake; instead, pull slices apart with 2 large forks. If you can find an angel food cake fork, so much the better, but they seem to have disappeared from the market.

❀ Tea Cake

total calories — 1076 • per serving — 135

The British can make quite a ceremony of high-tea service. Usually one is offered a choice of tea fragrances. There is also a trolley wagon of finger sandwiches and sweets. This glazed cake appears among the goodies. It is a rather simple cake containing no fat, but is always gilded with a bright red jelly glaze. Often this is the first cake to disappear from the cart.

Serves 8

2	eggs, room temperature	(154)
½	cup sugar, sifted	(385)
1	tablespoon hot water	——
2	teaspoons vanilla	(12)
1	cup sifted flour	(419)
½	teaspoon baking powder	(3)

GLAZE:

2	tablespoons red jelly — plum, currant, strawberry, or raspberry	(102)
¼	teaspoon kirsch or other white fruit alcohol	(1)

Preheat oven to 375°.

1. Warm a mixing bowl, break the eggs into it, and beat with a wire whisk or beater for 2 or 3 minutes. Add the sugar slowly, a few tablespoons at a time, beating well between each addition. Beat this sponge until it is very light and fluffy; it should take at least 5 minutes. Add the water and beat again for another 3 minutes, then add the vanilla.

2. Resift the flour with the baking powder and gently stir it into the batter. Select an 8-inch round nonstick cake pan. If using a regular cake pan, lightly grease it, fit the bottom with a round of wax paper, and lightly grease the paper; flour the pan and shake out excess. Scrape the batter into the pan and bake for 20 minutes, or until a toothpick plunged in the center comes out clean. Cool for 15 minutes on a rack, then remove the cake from the pan, carefully pull off the wax paper, and cool the cake completely.

3. To prepare the glaze, melt the jelly and kirsch together in a small pot or butter melter, then cool for a few minutes until the jelly just begins to thicken. Use a pastry brush to paint only the top of the cake with the glaze. Place the cake in the refrigerator for 10 minutes to set the glaze quickly. Remove from the refrigerator and keep the cake in a cool spot. Cut into wedges. (If you prefer not to glaze the cake, a dusting of powdered sugar can be substituted, again waiting until the cake is completely cool.)

❀ Spice Cake

total calories — 1211 • per serving — 151

Fortunately, Spice Cake is supposed to be spicy, not sweet. One expects the tang of the flavorings, which is too often overwhelmed with sugar. I think this cake strikes a happy balance.

Serves 8

1	cup sifted flour	*(419)*
3	tablespoons brown sugar	*(102)*
1½	teaspoons baking powder	*(8)*
½	teaspoon salt	——
1	teaspoon cinnamon	*(6)*
1	teaspoon nutmeg	*(11)*
½	teaspoon cloves	*(4)*
½	teaspoon ginger	*(3)*
3	eggs, separated, room temperature	*(231)*
1	egg white, room temperature	*(15)*
1	tablespoon water	——
1	teaspoon vanilla	*(6)*
1	tablespoon oil	*(120)*
¼	cup dark corn syrup	*(240)*
	pinch of cream of tartar	——
1	tablespoon granulated sugar	*(46)*

Preheat oven to 350°.

1. Resift the flour into a mixing bowl together with the brown sugar, baking powder, salt, cinnamon, nutmeg, cloves, and ginger. In a small bowl, beat together the egg yolks, water, vanilla, and oil. Pour the liquid over the dry ingredients and stir with a wooden spoon until blended. Add the syrup and stir again until the batter is smooth; it will be quite stiff.

2. Add the cream of tartar to the 4 egg whites and beat until they hold a peak. Sprinkle on the granulated sugar and beat again until the whites are quite firm.

3. Scoop about one-third of the whites over the batter and fold in quite well to lighten the batter. Scrape in remaining beaten whites and fold in delicately with a rubber spatula until evenly distributed. Do not overmix. Use an 8 × 8-inch nonstick cake pan,

or lightly grease a regular pan, line the bottom with wax paper, grease the paper, and flour the pan; shake out excess. Scrape the batter into the pan, tap the pan a few times on the table to settle the batter into the mold, and smooth the top wih a rubber spatula.

4. Place in the preheated oven and immediately turn down the heat to 325°. Bake for 45 to 50 minutes, or until a toothpick plunged in the center comes out clean. Cool for about 30 minutes, then carefully remove the cake from the pan and allow to cool completely before icing or cutting.

❀ Chocolate Cake

total calories — 1185 • per serving — 148
with icing — 183

Dark and luscious chocolate cake doesn't have to depend on calorie-rich chocolate for its flavor and color. Cocoa can do the job equally well, while sparing the calories contained in chocolate's cocoa butter. This chocolate cake is good enough to serve with only a powdered sugar coating, but for more festive occasions it can be covered with Chocolate Icing (page 201). The cake rises high enough to allow for slicing in half and filling with any of the compatible creams or icings in the book, or perhaps just a sprinkling of rum to spark the interior.

Serves 8

4	*eggs, room temperature*	*(308)*
¾	*cup sugar, sifted*	*(577)*
1	*teaspoon vanilla*	*(6)*
½	*cup flour*	*(224)*
¼	*teaspoon salt*	——
⅓	*cup cocoa*	*(70)*
¼	*teaspoon cream of tartar*	——

Preheat oven to 325°.

1. Separate the eggs into two large mixing bowls. Begin beating the yolks with an electric beater and gradually add the sugar, a few tablespoons at a time. Beat until the mixture is thick and lemon-colored. Add the vanilla and beat for another minute.

2. Sift together the flour, salt, and cocoa and gradually add to the beaten yolks; the batter will be quite stiff.

3. Add the cream of tartar to the egg whites and beat until they are stiff but not dry. Gradually incorporate the beaten whites into the batter; it is best to blend in only one-quarter at a time. The batter will gradually become quite supple, allowing the last half of the whites to be folded in gently.

4. Select a round 9-inch nonstick cake pan or lightly grease a regular pan. Fit a circle of wax paper on the bottom, grease it lightly, then flour the pan and shake out the excess. Spoon the batter into the pan, smooth the top with a spatula, and tap the pan gently on the table to settle the batter into the mold. Bake for 25 to 30 minutes, or until a toothpick plunged in the center comes out clean. Cool for 10 minutes on a rack, invert the cake, and gently pull off the wax paper. Turn the cake right side up and allow it to cool completely on the rack.

❁ Gâteau aux Poires
(Pear Cake)
total calories — 1309 • per serving — 164

This is a very pretty, though simple, cake that needs no adornment other than a light sprinkling of confectioners' sugar. The pears render a good deal of juice during the baking, giving the cake interior a slight custardy consistency that plays nicely against the crisp topping.

Serves 8

2	*eggs plus 1 yolk*	(216)
1	*cup skimmed milk*	(88)
2	*teaspoons vanilla*	(12)
¼	*teaspoon nutmeg*	(3)
1	*cup flour*	(455)
⅓	*cup sugar*	(230)
¼	*teaspoon salt*	——
1	*teaspoon baking powder*	(5)
3	*pears*	(285)
½	*tablespoon confectioners' sugar*	(15)

167

Preheat oven to 375°.

1. Beat together in a bowl the eggs, egg yolk, skimmed milk, vanilla, and nutmeg. Sift the flour with the sugar, salt, and baking powder and gradually add to the liquid ingredients. Pour the batter into a deep 9-inch pie dish.

2. Peel the pears, cut in half lengthwise, and remove the cores and seeds. Place the pears in a circle in the batter, cut sides down and with the stem ends toward the center. Do not allow the bottom ends to touch the sides of the dish. The rounded sides of the pears will be above the batter level.

3. Place in the oven and bake for about 35 minutes, or until the top is a deep golden brown and the pears are tender when pierced with a small, sharp knife. The batter will have puffed nicely. Pear Cake is to be eaten warm or cool, but it will shrink slightly as it cools. Sprinkle with the confectioners' sugar just before serving.

❀ Orange Upside-Down Cake

total calories — 1344 • per serving — 134

Every bit of the goodness of the fresh orange is used to flavor the cake batter as well as the bright gilding on top. Orange water replaces some of the sugar and butter usually lavished on the coating, all for the better in both flavor and calorie count.

Serves 10

1	medium navel orange	(64)
3	tablespoons brown sugar	(102)
1	tablespoon butter	(102)

BATTER:

3	tablespoons butter, room temperature	(306)
⅓	cup granulated sugar	(230)
1	egg	(77)
1	teaspoon vanilla	(6)
¼	teaspoon cinnamon	(2)
1	cup sifted flour	(419)

1¼ teaspoons *baking powder*	(6)
½ teaspoon *salt*	
⅓ cup *skimmed milk*	(30)

Preheat oven to 350°.

1. Rinse the orange, slice thin, and place in a pot. Pour in just enough water to cover the slices, bring to a boil, put a lid on top, and simmer about 15 minutes, or until the rinds are completely soft. Place a strainer over a bowl and pour the cooked oranges and their water into the strainer. Leave to drip thoroughly. Reserve the orange water.

2. Select an 8- or 9-inch-square cake pan and sprinkle in the brown sugar. Add the butter and 2 tablespoons of the orange water. Place the pan in the oven to melt the butter and sugar. Stir with a fork to spread the syrup evenly in the pan. Put aside.

3. Prepare the batter: Cream together the butter and granulated sugar. Add the egg, vanilla, cinnamon, and 2 tablespoons of orange water and beat well. Resift the flour with the baking powder and salt and add to the creamed ingredients alternately with the milk. Begin and end with the dry ingredients.

4. Arrange the cooked orange slices in rows in the syrup at the bottom of the cake pan. Place the slices side by side or overlapping, but do not allow them to touch the sides of the pan. Spoon the batter over the oranges carefully so as not to disturb the pattern. Smooth the batter into an even layer with a rubber spatula. Bake about 30 minutes, or until a toothpick plunged in the center comes out clean. Remove the cake and allow it to cool for 10 minutes. Reverse the cake onto the serving platter and allow to cool completely.

❈ Lemon Upside-Down Cake

total calories — 1555 • per serving — 156

Once boiled in water, the astringency of lemon disappears. Its natural tangy flavor does remain, making it a perfect foil for the spice cake beneath. That pronounced lemony accent should not be disguised with too thick a sugar topping. The amount indicated below blends in perfectly.

Serves 10

1	lemon	(20)
4	tablespoons brown sugar	(136)
2	tablespoons butter	(204)

BATTER:

1	cup sifted flour	(419)
3	tablespoons brown sugar	(102)
1½	teaspoons baking powder	(8)
½	teaspoon salt	——
1	teaspoon cinnamon	(6)
1	teaspoon nutmeg	(11)
½	teaspoon ginger	(3)
3	eggs, separated, room temperature	(231)
1½	teaspoons vanilla	(9)
1	tablespoon oil	(120)
¼	cup dark corn syrup	(240)
	pinch of cream of tartar	——
1	tablespoon granulated sugar	(46)

1. Boil the lemon for 20 minutes in a small pot with enough water to cover it by 1 inch. Lift the lemon out of the water and allow it to cool. Reserve ¼ cup of the lemon water. Slice the lemon thin and remove any seeds.

Preheat oven to 350°.

2. Measure into an 8-inch-square pan the 4 tablespoons of brown sugar, the butter, and 1 teaspoon of the lemon water. Place the pan in the oven to melt the butter and sugar; stir to distribute the topping evenly and put aside to cool.

3. Resift the flour in a mixing bowl together with the 3 table-spoons of brown sugar, the baking powder, salt, cinnamon, nut-meg, and ginger. Beat together in a small bowl the egg yolks, vanilla, oil, and 3 tablespoons of the lemon water. Pour the liquid into the mixing bowl and stir with a wooden spoon to moisten the dry ingredients thoroughly. Add the syrup and stir again until the batter is smooth; it will be quite stiff.

4. Add the cream of tartar to the egg whites and beat until they hold a peak. Sprinkle on the granulated sugar and beat again until the whites are firm.

170

5. Scoop about one-third of the whites over the batter and fold in well to lighten the batter. Scrape in the remaining beaten whites and fold in delicately with a rubber spatula to distribute them evenly.

6. Carefully arrange the lemon slices in the sugar topping prepared in the pan. Two or three parallel rows make an effective pattern. Gently spoon the batter over the lemon slices, taking care not to disturb the slices. Smooth the top of the batter with a rubber spatula and tap the pan on the table once or twice to settle the batter well into the pan. Bake for about 45 minutes, or until a toothpick plunged in the center comes out clean. Cool for about 10 minutes, then reverse the cake onto a serving dish.

✿ Tangy Wheat Germ Cake

total calories — 1272 • per serving — 159

The tang of this dusky cake comes from yogurt, which also helps insure a moist interior. Though not immediately identifiable, the toasted wheat germ adds a crunch and an intriguing hint of a nut flavor.

Serves 8

½	cup dark brown sugar	(272)
3	tablespoons oil	(360)
2	teaspoons vanilla	(12)
2	tablespoons carob powder	(54)
1	egg	(77)
½	cup plain low-fat yogurt	(64)
¾	cup flour	(336)
1	teaspoon baking powder	(5)
¼	cup toasted wheat germ	(92)
1	teaspoon baking soda	——

Preheat oven to 350°.

1. Stir together in a mixing bowl the brown sugar, oil, vanilla, and carob powder. Add the egg and yogurt and beat well to blend all the ingredients thoroughly. Gradually stir in the flour and

baking powder. When the flour has been completely incorporated, stir in the wheat germ and finally the baking soda.

2. Select an 8 × 8–inch nonstick cake pan or lightly grease a regular pan. Scrape the batter into the pan and smooth the top. Bake for about 20 minutes, or until a toothpick plunged in the center comes out clean.

❀ Basic Cake Roll

total calories — 1058 • per serving, without filling — 106

For anyone following calorie counts carefully there appear to be two discrepancies in the numbers listed below. First of all, the butter — although two tablespoons are indicated, the calorie count is for only one. That is because only the tablespoonful used to grease the paper actually touches the batter. Also, there is no specific quantity given for the confectioners' sugar, because even though it is sprinkled onto the towel liberally, no more than a tablespoon adheres to the cake itself. Other than that, sugar and flour calories have been trimmed a little from the classic recipe. Since the batter itself contains no butter, it is one of the lighter cakes around.

Serves 10

2	tablespoons soft butter or margarine	(102)
4	eggs, separated, room temperature	(308)
½	cup sugar	(385)
2	teaspoons vanilla	(12)
⅔	cup cake flour, sifted	(218)
¾	teaspoon baking powder	(4)
¼	teaspoon salt	——
	pinch of cream of tartar	——
	confectioners' sugar	(29)

Preheat oven to 375°.

1. Prepare a 12 × 16–inch cookie pan (not sheet) by greasing with 1 tablespoon butter. Line the pan with a sheet of parchment or wax paper that will extend about 4 inches beyond the ends.

The extra length will facilitate removal from the pan. Grease the wax paper with the remaining tablespoon of butter.

2. Beat the egg yolks in a mixing bowl until a pale yellow. Sift the sugar and add gradually to the yolks while continuing to beat. Add vanilla and beat again.

3. Resift the flour with the baking powder and salt and gradually add to the batter, beating well between additions; the batter will be quite stiff.

4. Add the cream of tartar to the egg whites and beat until stiff. Thoroughly mix about one-third of the beaten whites into the batter to lighten it. Carefully fold in the remaining whites just until blended; do not overmix. Spread the batter evenly in the prepared pan and place in oven for 11 to 13 minutes, or until the top springs back when pressed.

5. While the cake is baking, spread a large dish towel flat and sprinkle liberally with confectioners' sugar. Invert the cake on the towel, lift off the cookie pan, then carefully pull away the wax paper. Cut off the hard edges, lift one of the long sides, and roll up jelly-roll-fashion, pushing with the towel. Put aside until ready to fill, placing the seam side down. (If the filling is ready, it can be spread on before rolling.)

6. To fill: Unroll the cake and spread with ¾ cup of any of the fillings on pages 191 to 194. Reserve ⅓ cup of the filling to spread on top of roll, or just sprinkle with confectioners' sugar when serving. Spread the filling to within about ½ inch of the edge on three sides, and to within about 1 inch on the long seam side. Reroll, scraping away any filling that seeps from the seam side or the edges and add to the reserved filling. Just before serving, spread the reserved filling over the top of the roll and decorate with sliced fruit, mint sprigs, or fresh flowers. Slice on an angle with a serrated bread knife.

❀ Orange Roll Delight

total calories — 629 • *per serving — 63*

This delectable orange pastry is Portuguese in inspiration, but without the overwhelming sweetness Latin countries seem to favor. By cutting down sugar and adding a hint of cornstarch, more than half the calories have been saved without sacrificing any of the delicate texture and flavor. This is not a large, puffy roll, but more a dainty, custardlike confection. It is not advisable to refrigerate the dessert, because some of its lightness would be lost. Please follow the directions precisely. It really is quite simple to put together, with only a few steps and even fewer rules. But rules they are.

10 1-inch slices

2	*tablespoons soft butter or margarine*	*(102)**
3	*eggs, room temperature*	*(231)*
⅓	*cup granulated sugar, sifted*	*(230)*
1	*teaspoon cornstarch*	*(10)*
1	*teaspoon grated orange rind*	———
¼	*cup orange juice*	*(27)*
2	*tablespoons confectioners' sugar*	*(29)**
	Optional: Candied Orange Peel (page 43) for garnish	

Preheat oven to 325°.

1. Grease a 15 × 10 × 1–inch jelly-roll pan with 1 tablespoon butter. Place a sheet of parchment paper (not wax paper) on the sheet and fit it well into the edges and corners. Smear the paper with the remaining tablespoon of butter, making certain that the edges are also greased.

2. Break the eggs into a mixing bowl and beat with an electric beater until light and fluffy. Gradually add the granulated sugar, beating well between each addition. Sprinkle on the cornstarch and continue beating for another 5 or 6 minutes, or until the mixture almost quadruples in volume; it should be very thick and a pale lemon color.

3. Stir the orange rind into the juice and pour into the bowl gradually, using a rubber spatula to fold the juice into the batter. Pour the batter into the prepared pan and smooth the surface into an even layer with the rubber spatula; if the batter is not of the same depth over the entire pan, some areas will bake faster than others. Place in the oven for about 20 minutes, or until the batter

* Only half the quantity is used in the roll.

174

has a light golden top and begins pulling away from the paper.

4. While the pastry is baking, spread out a dish towel and sprinkle the confectioners' sugar over it. Turn the baked orange sheet upside down onto the towel and lift off the jelly-roll pan. Carefully pull off the parchment paper, using a small, dull knife to help release any stubborn patches (there won't be many, if any at all). Lift one of the long sides and roll the baked sheet jelly-roll-fashion. Rest the roll on its seam for at least 30 minutes before serving.

5. With a serrated knife cut off the hard ends diagonally. Cut the remaining roll into 1-inch diagonal slices. Garnish with the optional candied orange peel, if desired.

❋ Clafouti aux Pêches
(Peach Clafouti)

total calories — 1349 • per serving — 169

Clafouti is the funny name of a delicious hot dessert served in French homes. It most resembles a baked pancake with lots of fruit. Various produce of the season can be used, but cherries are traditional. Because a pound of fresh cherries has almost twice as many calories as peaches, it seemed wise to encourage the substitution. Strawberries would be another excellent possibility. If you would like to use the richer cherries, count an extra 18 calories per serving.

Serves 8

2 *tablespoons plus 1 teaspoon butter*	(238)
1 *pound peaches (about 4), peeled and sliced*	(131)
3 *eggs*	(231)
1 *cup skimmed milk*	(88)
2 *teaspoons lemon juice*	(2)
2 *teaspoons vanilla*	(12)
1 *cup flour*	(455)
¼ *cup sugar*	(192)

Preheat oven to 375°.

1. Slowly melt 2 tablespoons of butter while peeling and slicing the peaches. Grease a 6- or 7-cup pie dish or cake pan with the remaining teaspoon of butter and place the peaches in the pan. Do not press them into a compact layer; there should be enough space so the batter can seep around them.

2. Blend the eggs, melted butter, skimmed milk, lemon juice, and vanilla in the blender. Add the flour and sugar and process again. Pour this batter over the sliced fruit.

3. Place the baking dish in the oven and bake for about 30 minutes, or until the batter rises and puffs a little and a knife plunged into the center comes out clean. Serve hot or warm. Clafouti will shrink back into the dish somewhat as it cools. If it is to be served cold, sprinkle a small amount of powdered sugar over the surface just before serving.

❧ German Apple Pancake

total calories — 691 • per serving — 115

Many European countries have national versions of large fruit pancakes. In Germany it is usually apple that fills the baked dessert. The apples are sautéed on the stove top, covered with batter, and baked in the same skillet. The pancake emerges from the oven fragrant, hot, and puffy. The skillet is taken to the table at once. As soon as the pancake comes out of the oven, a sprinkling of cinnamon, or cinnamon mixed with sugar, is sometimes added, but this is not necessary. In the unlikely event that some of the delicious dessert is left over, remove it to a plate if your skillet is made of iron. The delicate pancake will absorb a metallic flavor if allowed to stand in the pan for any length of time.

Serves 6

2 medium apples	(106)
1 tablespoon butter	(102)
1 teaspoon plus 1 tablespoon sugar	(61)
1 teaspoon lemon juice	(1)
3 eggs	(231)

½ cup skimmed milk	(44)
pinch of salt	——
⅛ teaspoon nutmeg	(1)
1 teaspoon vanilla	(6)
⅓ cup flour	(140)

Preheat oven to 450°.

1. Peel, core, and slice the apples thin while melting the butter in a large skillet 10 to 12 inches in diameter. Add the apples, sprinkle with 1 teaspoon of sugar and the lemon juice, and sauté for a few minutes until the apples are a little tender and slightly translucent, about 2 or 3 minutes. Do not overcook the fruit at this point, because they will also be baked.

2. Beat the eggs in a mixing bowl, then stir in the milk, salt, nutmeg, vanilla, and the remaining 1 tablespoon of sugar. Finally, add the flour and beat until smooth.

3. Scatter the apples over the bottom of the skillet and pour the batter over them. Place in the hot oven for 15 minutes. Reduce the temperature to 350° and bake another 5 minutes. Test for doneness by piercing the center with a toothpick; it should be moist but have no batter clinging to it. Serve at once.

❀ Apples in Gilded Cages

total calories — 1242 • per serving — 207

One ounce of pastry dough turns the homeliest apple into this gilded beauty. A few strips of the dough are fashioned into a sort of peep-through corset around the fruit, all of which rests on a round of pastry. The combination is utterly beguiling and proves again that the better a dessert looks, the more we enjoy it. Pears can be treated the same way.

Serves 6

6 *medium apples, preferably Golden Delicious*	*(318)*
3 *to 4 cups water*	——
2 *tablespoons sugar*	*(92)*
strip of orange rind, about 2 inches long	——
2 *teaspoons vanilla*	*(12)*
1 *teaspoon cornstarch*	*(10)*
1 *teaspoon apple brandy*	*(4)*
1 *teaspoon apple jelly (not mint-flavored)*	*(17)*
1 *Pastry Dough recipe (page 158)*	*(746)*
2 *tablespoons evaporated milk*	*(43)*
Optional: 3 candied cherries cut in half or fresh green leaves, for garnish	

1. Pour 3 cups of water into an enameled or stainless-steel skillet, add the sugar, orange rind, and vanilla, and bring to the boiling point. Cover the skillet, reduce the heat, and allow the syrup to simmer. Meanwhile, peel the apples, leaving the stems intact and cutting off a thin slice from the bottom so they will stand up securely. Add the fruit to the syrup, which should reach a level halfway to two-thirds up the sides of the apples; if it doesn't, add more water. Cover the skillet and gently poach the apples until they are just soft when pierced with a small, sharp knife, about 20 minutes; turn them a few times during the cooking. Lift the apples out of the syrup with a slotted spoon and allow them to drain and cool.

2. During this time the sauce can be prepared. Measure 1 cup of the cooking syrup into a small pot. Mix 1 tablespoon of water into the cornstarch in a small bowl or cup and stir into the cooking syrup. Place on medium heat and add apple brandy and apple jelly. Cook until the sauce is slightly thickened, about the consistency of light cream. Remove from the heat and cool.

Preheat the oven to 400°.

3. Roll out the Pastry Dough to about ⅛-inch thickness. With a 3- or 3½-inch round scalloped cookie cutter, stamp out 6 circles and place them on a baking sheet. Place a well-drained apple on each circle. Cut the remaining dough with a fluted pastry wheel into ¼-inch-wide strips. Cut the strips into 3- to 4-inch lengths, depending on the height of the apples. Place 4 strips on

each apple, lengthwise from the stem to the bottom. Tuck the bottom end of each strip under the apple and press the fruit onto it. Wherever the pastry strips touch each other, wet the edges with water and press lightly. If the stems are long enough, wind the ends of the pastry strips around them. If you like, gather up the remaining dough, roll out again, fashion into leaf shapes, and fasten them to the top. With a pastry brush, paint all the dough with the evaporated milk. Bake for 10 to 15 minutes, or until the pastry turns a dark golden color.

4. These gilded apples are best served warm or at room temperature, not chilled. They can be further embellished with candied cherry halves or fresh leaves tucked beside the stems. Pass the sauce separately.

❀ Strawberry Bonbons

total calories — 821 · per bonbon — 137

Each plump little pastry package holds a whole fresh strawberry that bakes in its own juice. A bit over an ounce of pastry dough is sufficient to dress up the berry in grand style.

Makes 6 bonbons

1	*Pastry Dough recipe (page 158)*	*(746)*
6	*strawberries, rinsed and hulled*	*(30)*
1½	*teaspoons sugar*	*(23)*
1	*tablespoon evaporated milk*	*(22)*

Preheat oven to 375°.

1. Roll out the pastry and cut into 6 5-inch rounds. It will be necessary to gather the dough and reroll it after cutting out the first few rounds. With a pastry brush, paint the entire surface of each round with water.

2. Place a strawberry in the center of each pastry. Use about ¼ teaspoon of sugar to sprinkle over each berry and on the pastry around it.

3. Gather up the dough around the berry and pleat it Chinese-

style (as for steamed *dim sum*), or fashion it as you like. Leave a small hole in the top to vent the steam while baking. Place the pastry-covered berries on a baking sheet and brush lightly with the evaporated milk.

4. Bake the bonbons for about 15 minutes, or until the pastry turns a light honey color. Serve warm or cooled.

❀ Blueberry Grunt

total calories — 1217 • per serving — 152

Depending on where you come from, you might also call this homespun dessert a Buckle, Slump, or even Cobbler. All are based on a biscuit topping over simmering fruit. The batter should not be made ahead of time, but is best prepared while the berries are in the oven for their preliminary poaching.

Serves 8

3	cups blueberries	(270)
2	tablespoons brown sugar	(68)
½	teaspoon cinnamon	(3)
½	teaspoon nutmeg	(6)
1	tablespoon lemon juice	(4)
¼	cup orange juice	(27)
1	cup flour	(455)
1½	teaspoons baking powder	(8)
¼	teaspoon salt	——
2	tablespoons butter, chilled	(204)
2	eggs	(154)
1	teaspoon vanilla	(6)
2	tablespoons skimmed milk	(12)
	Optional: Whipped Topping (page 203) or Creamy Dessert Sauce (page 195)	

Preheat oven to 375°.

1. Rinse berries, picking off any stems, and pour them into a deep pie dish. Stir together the sugar, cinnamon, nutmeg, lemon

juice, and orange juice and pour over the berries. Place in the oven for about 10 minutes, or until the berries begin giving off their juice.

2. Meanwhile, mix the batter. Sift together into a bowl the flour, baking powder, and salt. Cut the butter in with a pastry cutter or two knives until the flour looks mealy. Beat together the eggs, vanilla, and milk and pour over the flour. Stir with a fork to blend the ingredients together, but do not beat until smooth.

3. As soon as the berries are removed from the oven, turn the heat up to 425°. Scrape the batter over the hot berries and, using a fork, spread the batter lightly so it completely covers the fruit. Return to oven for 15 to 20 minutes, or until the biscuit topping is puffed and golden brown. Serve hot, passing optional Whipped Topping or Creamy Dessert Sauce, if desired.

✿ Waffles

total calories — 763 • per waffle — 95

Hot waffles can be an extremely versatile base for all sorts of toppings — sliced fresh fruit, poached fruit, low-calorie sauces, syrups, and frozen fruit yogurts. The diet hazard of waffles is that usually the batter is heavily laced with butter, producing a calorie count that begins around 210 and zooms upward. Then the problem is compounded by sticky, sweet sauces that are poured over; that's double trouble. Here are waffles to eat with a clear conscience. Each weighs in with only 95 calories, and even with two tablespoons of one of the sauces or fillings in this book (Rum, Chocolate, Orange, Coffee Cream, Vanilla Pastry Cream), it will still only total up to between 125 and 145 calories.

Many recipes call for separating the eggs and adding beaten whites just before the baking. I have found this an unnecessary extra step. Beaten whites do a splendid job of puffing up a batter that is baked free-form, like pancakes, but once squeezed between the grids of a waffle iron, the extra air turns into steam. On the other hand, at least an hour's resting time for the batter is essential. This allows the gluten in the flour to soften and absorb the liquid, producing a thicker batter. Once cool, these waffles can be wrapped and frozen; reheat in a warm oven.

Makes 2 cups batter (8 waffles)

1¼	cups sifted cake flour	(436)
1½	teaspoons baking powder	(8)
1	tablespoon sugar	(46)
	pinch of salt	——
1	egg	(77)
1	teaspoon vanilla	(6)
1	cup skimmed milk	(88)
1	tablespoon butter, melted	(102)

1. Resift the flour, baking powder, sugar, and salt into a mixing bowl. Beat together in another small bowl the egg, vanilla, and skimmed milk. Gradually pour the liquid ingredients into the flour and stir with a wooden spoon to blend well. Do not overwork the batter; it should remain a little lumpy. Finally, stir in the melted butter. Cover the bowl and put aside for at least 1 hour.

2. Heat the waffle iron. Scrape every bit of the batter into a pitcher and when the iron is ready, pour in enough batter to cover two-thirds of the iron's surface. Close the cover and bake until most of the steam has stopped escaping from around the sides of the iron. Remove the baked waffles at once and keep warm in a low oven until the next batch is finished.

✱ Chocolate Waffles

total calories — 766 • per waffle — 96

These light brown waffles are especially good with either the Chocolate or Rum sauces, or the Coffee Cream Filling or Vanilla Pastry Cream in this book. A sprinkling of cocoa over the top heightens the chocolatiness, as well as looking attractive.

Makes 2 cups batter (8 waffles)

1¼	cups sifted cake flour	(436)
1½	teaspoons baking powder	(8)
1	tablespoon brown sugar	(34)
2	teaspoons cocoa	(10)
	pinch of salt	——
1	egg	(77)
1½	teaspoon vanilla	(9)
½	teaspoon rum	(2)
1	cup skimmed milk	(88)
1	tablespoon butter, melted	(102)

Follow directions in preceding recipe for Waffles, but add the cocoa to the sifted ingredients and add the rum to beaten liquid ingredients.

❀ Orange Waffles

total calories — 807 • per waffle — 101

Here is a sunny sort of waffle that could be a welcome addition to the Sunday brunch table, as well as to your dessert repertoire. Garnish them with poached oranges, Orange or Ginger Sauce, or Vanilla Pastry Cream. The slightly sharp Ginger Sauce, though, is best reserved for dinnertime.

Makes 2 cups batter (8 waffles)

1¼	cups sifted cake flour	(436)
1½	teaspoons baking powder	(8)
1	tablespoon sugar	(46)
	pinch of salt	——
1	egg	(77)
1	teaspoon vanilla	(6)
½	cup skimmed milk	(44)
½	cup orange juice	(54)
1	tablespoon plus 1 teaspoon butter, melted	(136)
	rind 1 orange, grated	——

Follow directions for Waffles (page 182). Add the orange juice to the beaten liquid ingredients and stir the grated orange rind into the batter after adding the melted butter.

✿ Pâte à Choux
(Cream Puff Pastry)

total calories — 1146 • *per 1½-inch shell — 24*
per 3-inch shell — 82

At first I didn't believe it. But I tried again and again, and it always worked. It *is* possible to make cream puff pastry with half the amount of butter usually specified. It is the eggs and the water that produce the expansion under high heat, not the fat. These baked shells are like all others — light and crisp. The same pastry is also used for making éclairs. Cream puff pastry is very easy to do, and since the finished puffs freeze well, a ready supply can be kept on hand for filling on the spur of the moment. Try the various fillings on pages 192 to 194. Especially good are the Pineapple, Strawberry, and Lemon, or the Vanilla Pastry Cream. A whole plump strawberry would make a particularly attractive summertime garnish.

Makes about 48 1½-inch shells or 14 3-inch shells

1	cup water	——
¼	cup butter, room temperature, cut into pieces	(408)
½	teaspoon sugar	(8)
½	teaspoon vanilla	(3)
	pinch of salt	——
1	cup sifted all-purpose flour	(419)
4	eggs, room temperature	(308)
	Optional: ¼ cup evaporated skimmed milk for glazing tops	(48)

Preheat oven to 425°.

1. In a heavy pot, boil together the water, butter, sugar, vanilla, and salt. Have the flour ready in a bowl or dish and as soon as

the butter has melted, dump the flour in all at once. It is important not to add the flour gradually. Reduce the heat and immediately begin beating with a wooden spoon until the batter forms a ball and pulls away from the sides of the pot. Continue beating over medium heat for another half-minute. Put aside to cool for 5 minutes.

2. Make a depression in the center of the batter with the wooden spoon and break an egg into it. Immediately beat this egg into the dough until it has been completely absorbed. At first the dough will look very shiny and slippery, but once the egg has been incorporated it will become duller. Repeat with the remaining eggs, one at a time.

3. It is best to use the pastry while still warm. Scoop it into a pastry bag fitted with a 1-inch round tip or use a teaspoon and a small rubber spatula. Place ¾- to 1-inch mounds of the pastry on a nonstick or lightly greased cookie sheet. Leave at least a ½-inch space between the rounds. The tiny points that remain on top when the dough is forced through the pastry bag can be smoothed by touching lightly with a wet finger. If a glazing is desired, brush the tops very lightly with the evaporated skimmed milk. Be careful to wipe away any milk that may dribble down the sides of the puff and onto the cookie sheet, for it will prevent rising. Place in the preheated oven for about 15 to 20 minutes, or until the pastry has puffed up and browned nicely. Turn off the oven, remove the cookie sheet, and shut the oven door.

4. Work quickly now. Puncture the side of each puff with a skewer or the tip of a small knife. Return the sheet to the oven for another 10 minutes, then open the door and allow to cool completely.

5. Cut off a cap from each puff and pull out the soft unbaked dough and discard. The shells can be filled immediately, or kept in an airtight container for up to a week. They can also be frozen, but when using, thaw them first and crisp in a 325° oven for about 5 minutes.

Coffee Meringue "Cake"

total calories — 810 • per serving — 135
serving with 2 tablespoons chocolate sauce — 179

Generally one sees meringue in the form of small puffs, or large shells for holding sweet fillings. In this recipe the frothy whites are baked in one mass that produces a crunchy base for sliced fresh fruit or a sauce, especially chocolate. Because of the addition of the coffee flavoring and the way the meringue is baked, a full ¾ cup of sugar (or half the usual amount) is dispensed with.

Serves 6

¾	*cup sugar*	*(577)*
½	*cup water*	——
6	*egg whites, room temperature*	*(90)*
½	*teaspoon cream of tartar*	*(1)*
2	*tablespoons plus 2 teaspoons instant coffee, preferably freeze-dried*	*(12)*
2	*teaspoons vanilla*	*(12)*
1	*tablespoon corn syrup*	*(60)*
2	*tablespoons cornstarch*	*(58)*
	hot Chocolate Sauce (page 196)	

Preheat oven to 325°.

1. In a small pot, boil the sugar and ¼ cup of water together for 5 minutes. (Have the remaining ¼ cup of water ready in a small cup.) Meanwhile, add the cream of tartar to the egg whites in a large mixing bowl and beat until the whites are very firm.

2. Pour the hot syrup over the egg whites while continuing to beat at a fast speed. Add the other ¼ cup of water and 2 tablespoons of instant coffee to the pot, and return it to high heat to dissolve the residual sugar clinging to its sides; swirl the pot to reach all surfaces.

3. Pour the dissolved coffee syrup over the whites while beating. Turn the speed to high and beat for 2 minutes more. Add the vanilla and corn syrup and beat again for another half-minute. Lightly fold in the cornstarch.

4. Oil an 8-cup soufflé* dish lightly and scoop the meringue into it. Tap the dish on the table a few times to settle the meringue well into it. Smooth the top with a spatula and sprinkle 2 teaspoons of instant coffee over it.

5. Put the soufflé dish in a pan containing 1 inch of hot water. Place the pan in the oven and bake for 45 minutes to 1 hour, or until the meringue puffs and begins pulling away from the sides. Remove from the oven and cool. The meringue will shrink somewhat.

6. To serve: Use two large spoons to cut portions of the meringue "cake" directly from the baking dish. Pass sliced fresh fruit or Chocolate Sauce.

❀ Crêpes

total calories — 914 • per crêpe — 38

Announce crêpes and everyone is instantly in a festive mood. There is no reason to forego this dessert delight just to remain within the bounds of low-calorie eating. The better it is made, the thinner it is, and in this low-calorie recipe each thin crêpe is a mere 38 calories. Even when gilded with any of the filling suggestions in the next recipe, the total amount still tips in on the very lean side.

Crêpes are most tender if they have not been chilled, which means making them the day they are to be served. They can be fried early in the day and will stay soft and mellow if the stack is covered with wax paper or plastic wrap and kept in a cool corner of the kitchen. Freeze them? You can do it, of course, but they won't be quite the same. The sauces, on the other hand, can be made in advance and refrigerated.

---

* The cake look can be heightened if the baked meringue is unmolded onto a serving platter; in this case, grease the soufflé dish a little more generously, using butter. Once cooled, the dessert can be carefully cut away from the sides of the dish with a thin knife, then eased out of the mold. Spoon several tablespoons of sauce over the top and pass the rest at the table.

Batter for 24 crêpes (7 to 8 servings)

1¼	cups flour	(567)
1	egg	(77)
½	teaspoon salt	——
2	teaspoons sugar	(30)
1½	cups lukewarm skimmed milk	(132)
1	teaspoon vanilla	(6)
1	tablespoon melted butter	(102)

1. Put the flour, egg, salt, sugar, milk, and vanilla in the blender and process until quite smooth. It may be necessary to scrape down the container with a rubber spatula to incorporate any thickened flour that adheres to the sides. Let the batter stand in the container for at least 30 minutes; an hour is better. Add the melted butter and process again.

2. Heat one or two nonstick crêpe pans measuring 5 to 6 inches in diameter. When hot, pour in about 3 tablespoons of batter and rotate the pan to cover the bottom with the batter. Pouring the batter from a pitcher facilitates and speeds up this step.

3. Fry each crêpe on one side for 1 to 1½ minutes. Shake the pan to loosen the crêpe, then turn it over with a spatula. Fry for a few seconds on the second side and slide the finished crêpe onto a plate. This will keep the first side up, which is prettier and the one always presented. Repeat with the rest of the batter. (If classic cast-iron crêpe pans are used, pour 1 tablespoon of oil into a small saucer, dip a cloth into it, and lightly wipe the pans between each frying; this will add 1 or 2 calories per crêpe.)

Always fill the side that was fried second; its coloring is not as even or attractive as the first side. Depending on the filling used, crêpes can be folded various ways. The most usual are:

Roll — after filling, roll cigar-fashion.

Long fold — fill and fold in thirds lengthwise.

Triangle — fill, fold in half, then lift the left edge and fold it over to meet the right edge.

❀ Crêpe Fillings

Below are just a few suggestions for crêpe fillings, but the possibilities are endless. Experiment with sliced fresh fruit, plain or mixed with a little sauce; it is always successful. Since every recipe in this book has been calorie-pared, try to rely on them for more elaborate presentations. For example, Ginger Pears (page 27) can be sliced thin and garnished with a bit of Ginger Sauce (page 198) and become an entirely new utilization of the fruit. Various pie fillings can be thinned with skimmed milk (or reduce the starch in the original cooking) and enormously expand your crêpe repertoire. Mix and match, be imaginative, and serve them often. They are inexpensive to make and endlessly adaptable.

Dessert crêpes should always be served warm. After filling and folding them, place them on a pie dish and heat in a 325° oven for 5 to 7 minutes.

Fillings for a single crêpe. (The calories noted are for the filling alone.)

Strawberries: Slice 3 strawberries and mix with 2 teaspoons Vanilla Pastry Cream (page 192). (31 calories)

Strawberry Cream Sauce (page 197): Spoon 1½ tablespoons down the center and fold in thirds, lengthwise. (15 calories)

Honey: Smear ½ teaspoon honey over the crêpe; mix together ¼ teaspoon brandy and 1 teaspoon evaporated skimmed milk. Pour half the liquid over the honey, fold the crêpe, and sprinkle the remaining liquid over the top. (18 calories)

Orange: Smear 1 tablespoon Orange Sauce (page 198) over the crêpe, fold, and garnish with a few strands of Candied Orange Peel (page 43). (17 calories)

Blueberries: Stir 1 tablespoon Ginger Sauce (page 198) into 2 tablespoons blueberries and spoon over the crêpe. (35 calories)

Coffee: Smear 1½ tablespoons Coffee Cream Filling (page 194) over the crêpe, sprinkle with ¼ teaspoon brandy or amaretto. (23 calories)

Banana: Simmer ¼ banana, sliced, in 3 tablespoons of orange juice until the banana just begins to soften. Place the fruit on the crêpe, fold, and sprinkle with the orange juice. (46 calories)

✻ Fillings, Sauces, Icings

A NUMBER OF RECIPES throughout this book include suggestions for sauces or fillings to be used with them. The rec-
ommendations, all in this chapter, are my personal preferences.
They may not agree with another cook's ideas. Please consider
this a mix-and-match section to select from according to your
fancy and taste. The sauces and fillings will not lead you astray
and confuse your calorie count. In most recipes the caloric figure
is given for each tablespoon, making it simple to figure how many
more calories are being added to embellish a cake or fruit mold,
or to top off a pie. For example, if a small cream puff (24 calories)
is garnished with pineapple filling (13 calories per tablespoon),
the total will be 37.

✻ Vanilla Pastry Cream

total calories — 4/8 • *per tablespoon — 24*

Wherever a recipe calls for traditional *crème patissière* you can
substitute this low-calorie cousin. The color, consistency, and
taste are quite the same — only the waistline knows the difference. This soft filling is especially useful for fruit tarts and cream
puff shells.

Makes 1¼ cups of pastry cream (enough to fill 7 or 8 4-inch tarts)

2	tablespoons cornstarch	(58)
	pinch of salt	——
2	tablespoons sugar	(92)
1	cup evaporated skimmed milk	(192)
1	egg, beaten	(77)
1	teaspoon vanilla	(6)
½	teaspoon of rum or liqueur — orange, cherry, or plum, depending on pastry flavor	(2)
½	tablespoon butter	(51)

1. In a heavy nonaluminum pot, stir together the cornstarch, salt, and sugar. Gradually add the evaporated skimmed milk, stirring with a whisk to keep the blend smooth. Make certain that the dry ingredients at the edges of the pot have been mixed in.

2. Place the pot on medium heat and stir until the mixture thickens. Have the egg ready in a mixing bowl and slowly pour in the hot sauce while whisking vigorously to keep the egg from curdling. With a rubber spatula, scrape every bit of the hot sauce into the bowl.

3. Return the sauce to the pot and place on low heat to cook for another half-minute, stirring constantly. Remove the pot from the heat and immediately add the vanilla and liqueur. Allow the sauce to cool slightly, then stir in the butter until it melts. Cover the sauce at once to keep a skin from forming. Cool, then chill until ready to use.

❀ Lemon Filling

total calories — 879 • per tablespoon — 22

Lemony desserts are universally popular, with good reason. That tangy citrus flavor can be counted on to perk up palates at the end of the meal. This filling would garnish one Basic Cake Roll (page 172), 50 1-inch Cream Puffs (page 184), or 14 to 16 4-inch tarts (pages 155 and 158). It would also be most compatible with Crêpes (page 188); for this use, reduce the cornstarch to 2 tablespoons and add only 1 egg.

Makes about 2½ cups of filling

¼	cup cornstarch	(116)
¾	cup sugar	(577)
1	cup water	——
½	cup lemon juice	(32)
	rind 1 lemon, grated	——
2	eggs	(154)

1. In a heavy saucepan, mix together the cornstarch and sugar. Gradually add the water, lemon juice, and lemon rind while stirring with a whisk. Place on a flame-deflector pad over medium heat and bring to a simmer. Reduce the heat, cover, and cook for 10 minutes, stirring occasionally.

2. Beat the eggs in a small bowl, pour in about half the hot filling, and beat together very well. Return the eggs and filling to the pot and cook about 2 minutes more over a slow fire, stirring constantly. Do not allow to boil. Remove from the fire and cool.

❀ Strawberry Filling

total calories — 481 • per tablespoon — 15

This is another filling that can be used in a number of ways — in Basic Cake Roll (page 172), Cream Puff shells (page 184), a full-sized pie (page 158), or small tarts (pages 155 and 158), or even to top off Meringue Puffs (page 140).

Makes 2 cups of filling

3	cups strawberries	(165)
⅓	cup sugar	(230)
2	tablespoons cornstarch	(58)
2	tablespoons orange liqueur	(24)
1	tablespoon lemon juice	(4)

Place berries in a heavy nonaluminum pot and mash. Add remaining ingredients and stir to blend thoroughly. Place on medium heat and bring to a simmer. Stir occasionally until the opaque filling turns translucent. Remove from heat and cool.

✿ Pineapple Filling

total calories — 599 • per tablespoon — 12

Makes 3 cups of filling

20-oz can crushed unsweetened pineapple, drained	(350)
3 tablespoons sugar	(138)
2 tablespoons kirsch	(24)
3 tablespoons cornstarch	(87)

Place all ingredients in a small, heavy pot. Place on a heat-deflector pad over low heat. Cook slowly and stir often until the mixture thickens, about 5 to 7 minutes. Remove from the heat and cool.

✿ Coffee Cream Filling

total calories — 269 • per tablespoon — 13

This is a recipe to keep in mind as a more unusual filling for Basic Cake Roll (page 172), as well as Cream Puff shells (page 184) and Chocolate Cake (page 166).

Makes 1¼ cups of filling

2 tablespoons cornstarch	(58)
pinch of salt	——
1 tablespoon instant coffee, preferably freeze-dried	(5)
1 tablespoon sugar	(46)
1 cup water	——
1 egg	(77)
1 tablespoon evaporated milk	(22)

194

1	teaspoon rum	(4)
1	teaspoon vanilla	(6)
½	tablespoon butter	(51)

1. In a heavy nonaluminum pot, stir together the cornstarch, salt, instant coffee, and sugar. Slowly add the water, stirring with a whisk to keep the blend smooth. Make certain that the dry ingredients at the edges of the pot have been mixed in.

2. Place the pot on medium heat and stir until the mixture thickens. Mix together in a bowl the egg, evaporated milk, and rum. Slowly pour in the hot sauce while whisking vigorously to keep the egg from curdling. With a rubber spatula, scrape every bit of the hot sauce into the bowl.

3. Return the sauce to the pot and place on low heat to cook for another half-minute, stirring constantly. Remove the pot from the heat and add the vanilla. Allow the sauce to cool slightly, then stir in the butter until it melts. Cover the hot sauce at once to keep a skin from forming. Cool, then chill until ready to use.

❄ Creamy Dessert Sauce

total calories — 556 • per tablespoon — 20

This mildly flavored sauce is especially compatible with caramel desserts such as Gossamer Caramel (page 60) and Caramel Apples (page 16), or any desserts containing chocolate or cocoa.

Makes approximately 1¾ cups of sauce

1	13-ounce can evaporated skimmed milk	(312)
3	tablespoons sugar	(138)
2	tablespoons cornstarch	(58)
⅓	cup skimmed milk	(30)
1	teaspoon vanilla	(6)
2	teaspoons orange liqueur	(88)
1	teaspoon brandy	(4)

Pour the evaporated skimmed milk into a small pot, add the sugar, and put on low heat. Mix the cornstarch and the skimmed milk to a smooth paste and slowly add to the hot milk while mixing with a wire whisk. Keep whisking until the sauce thickens, then add the vanilla, liqueur, and brandy. Simmer for 1 minute more. Chill.

❀ Chocolate Sauce

total calories — 654 • per tablespoon — 23

You will find this a very useful sauce for garnishing crêpes, custards, and molded desserts. By substituting cocoa for chocolate many calories have been whittled away.

Makes about 1¾ cups of sauce

¼	cup sugar	(192)
1	cup evaporated skimmed milk	(192)
3	tablespoons cocoa	(42)
2	tablespoons butter	(204)
2	teaspoons vanilla	(12)
1	tablespoon rum	(12)

Put all ingredients in the blender and blend for 1 minute. Pour the sauce in a small saucepan and bring to a slow simmer. Cook for 1 minute. This Chocolate Sauce may be served hot or cold.

❀ Strawberry Sauce

total calories — 278 • per tablespoon — 17

Makes about 1 cup of sauce

1	pint strawberries	(121)
3	tablespoons sugar	(144)
1	teaspoon lemon juice	(1)
1	teaspoon orange liqueur	(12)

Put all ingredients in an electric blender or food processor and purée until smooth. Lacking either of the electric machines, put the berries through a food mill and stir in the sugar, lemon juice, and orange liqueur. Refrigerate the sauce for at least 2 hours before serving.

✺ Strawberry Cream Sauce

total calories — 326 • per tablespoon — 10

Makes approximately 2 cups of sauce

1	cup strawberries	(55)
¼	cup orange juice	(27)
1	teaspoon lemon juice	(1)
1	tablespoon cornstarch	(29)
2	tablespoons sugar	(92)
	pinch of salt	——
½	cup evaporated skimmed milk	(96)
¼	cup skimmed milk	(22)
1	teaspoon orange liqueur	(4)

1. Purée together the strawberries, orange juice, and lemon juice in an electric blender or food processor.

2. Measure into a heavy enameled saucepot the cornstarch, sugar, and salt and stir with a wooden spoon to blend the dry ingredients. Pour in the purée while stirring to keep the sauce smooth. Finally, stir in the evaporated and fresh skimmed milks and the orange liqueur.

3. Place the pot on medium heat and cook while stirring until the sauce thickens, about 2 or 3 minutes. Remove from the fire, cool, then chill.

❀ Orange Sauce

total calories — 276 • per tablespoon — 17

Makes 1 cup of sauce

2 tablespoons cornstarch	*(58)*
1 tablespoon sugar	*(46)*
rind of 1 orange, grated	——
1 cup orange juice	*(110)*
1 egg yolk	*(62)*

1. In a heavy nonaluminum pot, stir the cornstarch, sugar, and orange rind together. Gradually pour in the orange juice while stirring with a whisk to keep the mixture smooth. Place on a medium fire and cook, stirring constantly, until the liquid thickens, about 3 or 4 minutes.

2. Have the egg yolk ready in a small mixing bowl and beat it as the hot sauce is slowly poured in. Scrape all the sauce from the pot into the bowl, then put the contents of the bowl back into the pot and return to the heat for a half-minute while continuing to beat. Remove from the heat, cool, then chill.

❀ Ginger Sauce

total calories — 548 • per tablespoon — 23

Makes approximately 1½ cups of sauce

1 13-oz. can evaporated skimmed milk	*(312)*
1 tablespoon cornstarch	*(29)*
½ teaspoon ground ginger	*(3)*
2 tablespoons honey	*(128)*
2 tablespoons brown sugar	*(68)*
2 teaspoons rum	*(8)*

Pour 1 cup of the milk into a small, heavy pot. In a small cup or bowl, stir the remaining milk into the cornstarch and add it to the pot. Add all other flavoring ingredients and cook over low heat until the sauce thickens, about 5 minutes. Keep stirring with a wire whisk to prevent any lumps from forming. Cool, then chill.

❀ Rum Sauce

total calories — 438 • per tablespoon — 18

Makes approximately 1½ cups of sauce

1	13-ounce can evaporated skimmed milk	*(312)*
1½	tablespoons cornstarch	*(44)*
2	tablespoons brown sugar	*(68)*
1	tablespoon dark rum	*(12)*
½	teaspoon brandy	*(2)*

Pour 1 cup of the milk into a small, heavy pot. In a small cup or bowl, stir the remaining milk into the cornstarch and add it to the pot. Add all other flavoring ingredients and put the pot over low heat. Cook slowly until the sauce thickens, about 5 minutes. Keep stirring with a wire whisk to prevent any lumps from forming. Cool, then chill.

❀ Orange Glaze

total calories — 407 • per tablespoon — 25

This glaze is especially good with Angel Food Cake (page 162), but it could also fill Cream Puff shells (page 184), and small tarts (pages 155 and 158). For the last two, chill the glaze before using.

Makes 1 cup of glaze

3	tablespoons cornstarch	*(87)*
1	tablespoon sugar	*(46)*
	rind of 1 orange, grated	——
1	cup orange juice	*(110)*
1	egg yolk	*(62)*
1	tablespoon butter	*(102)*

1. In a heavy nonaluminum pot, stir the cornstarch, sugar, and orange rind together. Gradually pour in the orange juice while stirring with a whisk to keep the mixture smooth. Place on a medium fire and cook, stirring constantly, until the liquid thickens, about 3 or 4 minutes.

2. Have the egg yolk ready in a small mixing bowl and beat it as the hot sauce is slowly poured in. Scrape all the sauce from the pot into the bowl, then put the contents of the bowl back into the pot and return to the heat for a full minute, continuing to stir constantly. Do not allow it to come to a boil. Remove from the heat, cool for a minute, then stir in the butter until melted. Cool completely. As it cools, the glaze will thicken. Spread on cool cake, then chill to set. Once set, the cake can be removed from the refrigerator and kept in a cool spot.

❊ Butterscotch Icing

total calories — 369 • per tablespoon — 23

Makes 1 cup of icing (enough for top and sides of an 8-inch cake)

½ cup low-fat cottage cheese	(63)
2 ounces butterscotch morsels (about ⅓ cup)	(300)
1 tablespoon skimmed milk	(6)

Place the cottage cheese in the blender and process to smooth the curds. Put the butterscotch morsels and skimmed milk in a small, heavy pot over low heat. Stir until the candies have melted, then scrape into the blender. Process until the mixture is very smooth. Chill slightly before spreading on the cake.

❊ Strawberry Icing

total calories — 327 • per tablespoon — 14

When fresh strawberries are not available, substitute 8 ounces of frozen unsweetened berries.

Makes 1½ cups of icing

2 cups strawberries	(110)
1 tablespoon lemon juice	(4)
1 tablespoon kirsch	(12)

2 tablespoons cornstarch	(58)
2 tablespoons sugar	(92)
pinch of salt	——
½ cup water	——
½ tablespoon butter	(51)

1. In the container of an electric blender or food processor, place the berries, lemon juice, and kirsch and process until smooth.

2. In a heavy enameled saucepot, stir together the cornstarch, sugar, and salt. Slowly stir in the water, keeping the mixture smooth and free of lumps. Pour in the berry purée and place the pot on a heat-deflector pad over medium heat.

3. Stir while cooking the sauce until it thickens and turns translucent, then cover, reduce the heat, and cook for 2 minutes longer. Remove the pot from the heat, cool for 5 minutes, then stir in the butter to dissolve. Cool the icing a little before using.

✿ Chocolate Icing

total calories — 281

A superabundance of sugar, cream, and butter will drive most chocolate icings up to at least 1000 calories for a single 9-inch cake. Often the additions detract from the chocolatiness of the icing. This recipe strikes a nice balance.

Sufficient icing for top and sides of one 9-inch cake

1 ounce semisweet chocolate, broken in pieces	(144)
1 teaspoon rum	(4)
1 tablespoon evaporated skimmed milk	(12)
2 tablespoons (1 oz.) Neufchâtel (low-fat) cream cheese	(70)
½ tablespoon butter	(51)

1. Melt together in a small pot or butter melter the chocolate, rum, and skimmed milk. Keep the heat quite low and stir often; this should take only 2 or 3 minutes.

2. Meanwhile, in a small mixing bowl, beat the cream cheese

with a wooden spoon to soften it. Scrape in the melted chocolate and beat rapidly until thoroughly blended and fluffy. Stir in the butter until it has melted. Cool slightly, then spread on cake.

❀ Meringue Topping

total calories — 171

For one 9-inch pie

2 egg whites, room temperature	(30)
¼ teaspoon cream of tartar	——
3 tablespoons sugar, sifted	(138)
½ teaspoon vanilla	(3)

Preheat oven to 350°.
1. Add the cream of tartar to the egg whites and beat until they are stiff, but not dry. Add the sugar, a teaspoon at a time, then add the vanilla and beat only until it is blended into the meringue and the sugar has completely dissolved.
2. Spread the meringue over the warm pie filling. Make certain the topping reaches all the way to the crust. Bake for 10 to 15 minutes, depending on the thickness of the meringue.

❀ Whipped Topping

total calories — 314 • per tablespoon — 5

I think you will find this a particularly easy and dependable recipe for a whipped dessert topping. Unlike most low-calorie whipped "creams," this one does not have to be rushed to the table. In fact, it must be made ahead of time to allow the very small amount of gelatin to set. A blender cannot be used for this recipe, because it processes too fast and does not incorporate enough air into the mixture.

Makes about 4 cups of topping

1 teaspoon gelatin	(8)
6 tablespoons skimmed milk	(36)
½ cup ice water	——
½ cup skimmed milk powder	(218)
1 tablespoon sugar	(46)
1 teaspoon vanilla	(6)
few drops of lemon juice	——

1. Chill the bowl and beater thoroughly. Meanwhile, moisten the gelatin in 2 tablespoons of the skimmed milk. In a small pan, heat the remaining 4 tablespoons of skimmed milk, add the softened gelatin, and stir until it is completely dissolved. Set aside to cool and thicken a little.

2. The water must be very cold; I like to keep it in the freezer until ice crystals begin to form. Pour the ice water into the chilled bowl and add about 2 tablespoons of the skimmed milk powder. Begin beating at low speed, then beat for a half-minute at high speed. Return speed to low and continue adding the rest of the powder slowly. Increase speed to medium while adding the sugar, vanilla, and lemon juice. Turn to high speed, add the gelatin-milk mixture, and continue beating. Long beating, 7 to 10 minutes in all, is essential to incorporate as much air as possible into the topping. Scoop it into a serving bowl and refrigerate for at least 2 hours.

✻ Whipped Evaporated Milks

made with evaporated skimmed milk:
total calories — 136 • per tablespoon — 6
made with evaporated milk:
total calories — 212 • per tablespoon — 9

In various recipes throughout this book, directions are given for whipping canned evaporated milk and evaporated skimmed milk for incorporating into desserts. The whipped milks can also be used as an excellent topping to pass with hot or cold fruits, over cobblers and puddings, or to top off a piece of chocolate cake. Unlike the Whipped Topping (preceding recipe), which holds up for hours because it contains a bit of gelatin, these whips are to be served as soon as they are finished. The procedure for both milks is exactly the same; only the calorie count differs. Compare these figures with regular whipped cream — 30 calories per tablespoon. An electric hand beater is the best utensil for whipping; a blender cannot be used.

Makes 1½ cups of whipped milk

½ cup evaporated skimmed milk or evaporated milk	(96–172)
1 teaspoon lemon juice	(1)
2 teaspoons sugar	(30)
1½ teaspoons vanilla	(9)

Pour the milk into a medium-sized mixing bowl and place in the freezer with the beaters. Once ice crystals begin forming around the edges of the milk, in about 20 to 30 minutes, add the lemon juice and beat at high speed until the milk becomes fairly thick. Add the sugar, a teaspoon at a time, and when it is thoroughly incorporated, add the vanilla and beat for another half-minute. Scoop the whipped milk into a chilled bowl and serve at once.

Index

✻ Index